Solid Personal Finances

The Key to Achieving Financial Freedom and Leaving a Legacy

Ojeda

Copyright © 2024 Ojeda
All rights reserved.
ISBN: 9798344427195
Imprint: Independently published

Contenido

- Introduction: 1
- Chapter 1: The Power of Financial Mindset 3
  - How Your Beliefs Influence Your Economy 3
- Chapter 2: Organize Your Personal Finances 8
  - First Steps Toward Financial Stability 8
- Chapter 3: Creating an Effective Budget 15
  - Planning Every Euro Wisely 15
- Chapter 4: Eliminate Debt Smartly 21
  - Strategies to Get Out of Debt Without Extreme Sacrifices 21
- Chapter 5: Saving: The Key to Financial Well-Being 27
  - Simple Techniques to Save Effortlessly 27
- Chapter 6: Multiply Your Income with New Opportunities 33
  - Additional Income Sources to Improve Your Finances 33
- Chapter 7: Basic Investments for Beginner 41
  - How to Grow Your Money Safely 41
- Chapter 8: How to Protect Your Finances from the Unexpected ... 49
  - Planning for Unforeseen Events 49
- Chapter 9: Living Within Your Means 55
  - Controlling Expenses Without Sacrificing Quality of Life 55
- Chapter 10: Continuous Financial Education 61
  - The Importance of Continuing to Learn About Finance 61
- Chapter 11: The Impact of Taxes on Your Economy 67
  - Strategies to Optimize Your Taxes 67

Chapter 12: Plan Your Retirement Starting Today 75
    How to Ensure a Stable Economic Future 75

Chapter 13: How to Avoid Common Financial Mistakes 84
    What You Should Know to Avoid Economic Pitfalls 84

Chapter 14: Relationships and Money: A Crucial Balance 90
    How Money Affects Your Relationships and How to Manage It 90

Chapter 15: Building Your Financial Future: The Long-Term Plan 98
    Creating a Comprehensive Plan for Financial Security 98

Chapter 16: The Importance of Financial Legacy and Estate Planning 106
    How to Ensure Your Wealth Transcends Future Generations . 106

Chapter 17: The Importance of Financial Flexibility in Times of Uncertainty 113
    How to Adapt and Protect Your Finances in Difficult Times .. 113

Chapter 18: The Importance of Financial Independence and How to Achieve It 120
    How to Free Yourself from Financial Worries and Live on Your Own Terms 120

Chapter 19: Long-Term Wealth Preservation Strategies 129
    How to Protect and Grow Your Assets with a Future-Oriented Vision 129

Chapter 20: From Financial Security to Building a Lasting Legacy 137
    How to Ensure Your Wealth and Values Endure for Future Generations 137

Introduction:

In a world where the global economy is constantly changing and personal financial circumstances are becoming increasingly challenging, it is crucial to acquire the necessary tools and knowledge to improve and manage your personal finances. Regardless of your starting point, there is always room to improve your finances, achieve stability, and ultimately reach financial independence.

The purpose of this book is to offer you a clear and practical guide on how you can take control of your finances, regardless of your current situation. It doesn't matter if you are in debt, starting from scratch, or already have a certain level of financial stability; the principles you will find here will help you move toward a better financial position.

The foundation for economic success lies in understanding that your finances do not depend solely on the income you receive, but also on how you manage that income, how you plan for your future, and how you avoid the traps that often lead to bad financial habits. This book aims to demystify the financial management process, showing that anyone, regardless of their income level or prior knowledge, can improve their financial situation with the right steps.

In the first chapters, we will focus on fundamental aspects such as changing your mind-set toward money and understanding how your beliefs influence the way you handle your finances. Often, our financial habits are shaped by ideas and patterns we have adopted without even questioning them. Identifying and changing these patterns is the first step toward transformation.

Then, we will move on to organizing your personal finances. One of the biggest obstacles people face when trying to improve their financial situation is a lack of organization. Not knowing exactly how much money comes in and goes out each month, or not having clarity about financial priorities, can create a sense of being out of control. With a practical approach, you will learn how to organize your income and expenses in a way that allows you to make informed decisions.

The book also addresses topics such as the importance of budgeting, effectively eliminating debt, saving, investment opportunities for beginners, and how to protect yourself against unexpected events. Each of these topics will be addressed with examples and strategies that you can immediately apply to your life.

Beyond the technical aspects of finance, this book also covers a fundamental area that is often overlooked: the emotions and relationships surrounding money. How you manage your finances can significantly affect your personal relationships, and learning to balance these aspects is crucial for your overall well-being.

Finally, the goal is that, by the time you finish reading this book, you will not only have improved your current financial situation but will also have the tools and mind-set necessary to continue growing financially in the future. This is not just a financial survival manual; it is a guide to a fuller, more stable economic life, and, above all, one that is under your control.

Get ready to embark on a journey of financial transformation that will not only help you improve your finances but will also provide you with a sense of freedom and confidence to face any economic challenge that comes your way.

Chapter 1: The Power of Financial Mind-set

How Your Beliefs Influence Your Economy

One of the most overlooked truths about personal finance is the profound impact that our beliefs, attitudes, and mental patterns have on our ability to manage and improve our finances. Beyond numbers, balances, and budgets, financial success originates in the mind. People who achieve stability and prosperity do not do so solely because they earn more money but because they have adopted a mind-set that allows them to make wise and consistent decisions over time. This chapter delves into how your financial mind-set influences your economy and how you can start transforming it to reach your goals.

1.1. Limiting Beliefs: Identifying Internal Obstacles

From an early age, many of us absorb ideas and beliefs about money that, although we may not consciously notice, influence how we manage our finances. Often, these beliefs come from family, culture, or life experiences. Below are some of the most common limiting beliefs that affect many people:

"Money is the root of all evil": This saying, while popular, can lead to the belief that money is bad or corrupt. If we subconsciously associate money with evil, we may sabotage our opportunities to earn more or save.

"I'm not good at managing money": Many people believe they lack the necessary skills to handle their finances. This belief becomes a self-fulfilling prophecy, where a lack of confidence leads to poor management.

"I will never have enough money": This is a recurring thought that generates a scarcity mind-set. Those who experience it tend to focus on a lack of resources, which prevents them from seeing opportunities to generate income or improve their financial situation.

"To make money, you need money": Although it's true that capital can facilitate investments, this belief can paralyze those who think they cannot improve their financial situation without a large sum of money to start with.

These limiting beliefs, when unrecognized and unaddressed, act as invisible barriers that hinder financial growth. The first step toward a healthy financial mind-set is identifying and replacing them with more positive and realistic thoughts.

1.2. Abundance Mind-set vs. Scarcity Mind-set

One of the keys to improving your finances is adopting an abundance mind-set instead of a scarcity mind-set. These two terms describe opposite ways of perceiving the world and, therefore, making financial decisions.

The scarcity mind-set is marked by fear, a constant worry that there are not enough resources for everyone. People with this type of mind-set focus on what they don't have, which often leads them to make financial decisions based on fear: spending more than they should, avoiding productive risks, or not seeking new opportunities for fear of losing what they already have.

On the other hand, those who adopt an abundance mind-set see the world as a place full of opportunities. They don't focus on what they lack but on what they can do to improve their situation. This mind-set does not mean ignoring difficulties but rather facing them with the confidence that there are solutions and opportunities to move forward.

Transforming your mind-set toward abundance doesn't happen overnight, but with practice and conscious attention, you can start changing your perception of money and the opportunities around you.

1.3. How Mind-set Impacts Your Financial Habits

Your mind-set toward money directly affects your financial habits. Here are some examples of how these beliefs and attitudes translate into behaviours:

Saving or spending: People with a scarcity mind-set tend to spend immediately what they earn, feeling that if they don't, something worse might happen. In contrast, those with an abundance mind-set value saving as an investment in the future.

Investments and risks: The scarcity mind-set often leads to avoiding investments or any kind of risk, for fear of losing money. In contrast, those who adopt an abundance mind-set understand that calculated risk is part of financial growth and are willing to invest in their future.

Debt: People with a scarcity mind-set often resort to debt as a short-term solution to their financial problems, without a clear strategy to get out of it. On the other hand, an abundance mind-set seeks to reduce debts and use credit wisely and strategically.

1.4. Strategies to Change Your Financial Mind-set

Transforming your financial mind-set is a process that requires time and dedication, but the results can be transformative. Here are some strategies to start with:

Reevaluate your beliefs about money: Take time to reflect on the ideas you have about money. Where do they come from? Are they helping or limiting you? Reframe negative beliefs with more positive and realistic thoughts.

Adopt positive financial affirmations: Affirmations are a powerful tool to reprogram your mind. Repeat daily affirmations like "I am capable of managing my money well" or "Opportunities to increase my income are all around me."

Surround yourself with people with an abundance mind-set: Mind-setss are contagious. If you surround yourself with people who see opportunities instead of obstacles, you too will begin to adopt a similar attitude. Seek mentors or peers who inspire you to improve your financial situation.

Focus on opportunities, not limitations: Instead of worrying about what you don't have, focus on what you can do with what you do have. Shift your focus toward creating solutions, not problems.

1.5. The Connection Between Gratitude and Prosperity

A key component of the abundance mind-set is gratitude. When you take the time to be grateful for what you already have, you train your brain to focus on the positive rather than the negative. This simple act not only makes you feel more content with your current situation but also opens your mind to new opportunities. Gratitude shifts your focus from lack to abundance, creating a mind-set conducive to prosperity.

Practicing gratitude daily, whether by writing in a journal or simply reflecting on what you are grateful for, can have a significant impact on your emotional and financial well-being.

Mind-set transformation is the first step toward financial success. Recognizing that your thoughts influence your economic decisions is key to reprogramming your financial habits and beginning to build a more prosperous financial future. With this foundation, you are ready to move on to the more practical aspects of financial organization, which we will explore in the next chapter.

Chapter 2: Organize Your Personal Finances

First Steps Toward Financial Stability

One of the most important keys to achieving financial stability is organization. Without a clear control over your income and expenses, it is easy to fall into habits that can negatively affect your finances. Often, financial stress doesn't stem from a lack of money but from a lack of organization and planning. In this chapter, you will learn the essential first steps to organizing your personal finances and start building a solid foundation for your financial future.

2.1. Financial Diagnosis: Knowing Your Current Situation

Before making any changes or improvements to your finances, it is crucial to have a clear and precise idea of your current situation. This is the first step to achieving financial stability: conducting a financial diagnosis.

A financial diagnosis involves a detailed analysis of your income, expenses, debts, and assets. The following are the key elements you should analyze:

Income: Make a detailed list of all your income sources. This includes your salary, additional income such as side jobs, rentals, or investments. It's important to have a clear understanding of the monthly amount you receive from each source.

Expenses: This is where most people tend to have less clarity. Separate your expenses into categories, such as housing, transportation, food, entertainment, health, among others. Be sure to include both fixed expenses (such as rent or utility bills) and variable ones (like food, leisure, shopping). It is recommended to do this for a full month to get a clear view of where you are spending your money.

Debts: Make a list of all the debts you have. Include personal loans, credit card debts, mortgages, and any other type of debt. Specify the total amount owed, the interest rate, and the term for each of them.

Assets: Assets are the items you own that have value, such as properties, savings, investments, or vehicles. Make a list of these assets and their approximate value. Knowing your assets will help you have a clear idea of your net worth.

The goal of this diagnosis is to have a complete picture of your financial situation. Many people avoid doing this analysis out of fear of what they will find, but it's impossible to improve what is not measured. Knowing your current situation is the first step toward taking control.

2.2. Creating a Budget: The Pillar of Financial Organization

Once you've made your financial diagnosis, the next step is to create a budget. A budget is an essential tool for organizing your finances, as it allows you to consciously and controlledly allocate your income to different expense categories.

To create an effective budget, follow these steps:

Determine your net income: Make sure your budget is based on net income, that is, the money you actually receive after taxes and other deductions.

Set your essential expenses: Essential expenses are those you need to cover to maintain your daily life, such as housing, food, transportation, and health. These expenses should be prioritized in your budget.

Set an amount for savings: Before allocating money to non-essential expenses, set aside a portion of your income for savings. Ideally, you should save at least 10-20% of your income, but if that's not possible, start with what you can. The key is to do it consistently.

Create categories for variable expenses: Here you can include categories such as entertainment, clothing, technology, among others. The key is to allocate realistic amounts and not exceed the limit you have set.

Manage your debts: Make sure to include in your budget an amount to pay off your debts. If you have multiple debts, it is recommended to prioritize those with higher interest rates.

A tool you can use to simplify the process is the 50/30/20 rule:

- 50% for essential expenses.
- 30% for variable expenses or desires.
- 20% for savings and debt repayment.

This method provides you with a simple and easy-to-follow structure that will help you keep your finances under control without feeling overly restricted.

2.3. Setting Financial Goals

Once you have created your budget, it is important to set financial goals. Goals provide you with clear direction and motivate you to keep organizing your finances effectively. Financial goals can be short, medium, or long-term, and they should be SMART: specific, measurable, achievable, relevant, and time-bound.

Examples of financial goals include:

- Saving for an emergency fund of six months of expenses.
- Eliminating a credit card debt in the next year.
- Saving for the purchase of a house in five years.
- Investing a percentage of your income each month in a retirement fund.

Each of these goals should have a clear plan for how to achieve them, whether by increasing your income, reducing your expenses, or both. By defining specific goals, you will be able to better organize your finances in line with these priorities.

2.4. Tools to Organize Your Finances

In the digital age, there are numerous tools and applications that can help you organize your finances more efficiently. These tools can make the process of creating and following a budget simpler and more accessible. Here are some of the most recommended:

Budgeting apps: Tools like Mint, YNAB (You Need A Budget), or Fintonic allow you to connect your bank accounts and automatically track your expenses, income, and debts. Additionally, they provide charts and reports that help you visualize your financial situation.

Spreadsheets: If you prefer a more personalized approach, you can use tools like Google Sheets or Excel to create your own budgets and expense logs. This allows you to have more detailed control over how you organize your information.

Debt tracking apps: If you have multiple debts, tools like Debt Payoff Planner or Undebt.it help you organize your payments, prioritize debts, and create a plan to eliminate them effectively.

Using these tools will allow you to continuously track your financial situation and make real-time adjustments when necessary.

2.5. The Importance of an Emergency Fund

A fundamental aspect of financial organization is the creation of an emergency fund. This fund is a reserve of money that allows you to cover unexpected expenses, such as car repairs, unforeseen medical expenses, or even temporary loss of income.

An emergency fund should be accessible and liquid, meaning you can access it quickly when needed. Ideally, this fund should cover between three and six months of your essential expenses. While it may seem like a difficult goal to reach, it is crucial that you start small and gradually increase this fund over time. The peace of mind that comes with having a financial cushion for any unforeseen event is invaluable.

2.6. Continuous Monitoring and Control

Once you have established a budget and financial goals, it is essential to regularly monitor your finances. Financial organization is not something you do once, but it requires constant review and adjustments. Dedicate time each week or month to review your accounts, compare your expenses with the budget, and ensure you are on track to meet your goals.

Monitoring will also help you detect problems early, such as unnecessary expenses or accumulating debt, and take corrective action before they become bigger problems.

Organizing your personal finances is the first step toward a more stable and stress-free economic life. By diagnosing your current situation, creating an effective budget, setting clear goals, and using the right tools for monitoring and control, you will be on your way to better financial organization. With a solid foundation, you will be able to make more informed and strategic decisions to improve your economic situation in both the short and long term.

Chapter 3: Creating an Effective Budget

Planning Every Euro Wisely

One of the fundamental pillars for achieving financial stability is knowing how to create an effective budget. A budget is not just a simple spreadsheet where you jot down income and expenses; it is a strategic tool that allows you to have control over your finances, make informed decisions, and ensure that every euro you earn is well allocated. This chapter will provide you with the necessary guidelines to plan every euro intelligently, maximizing your resources and helping you reach your financial goals.

3.1. What is a Budget and Why is it Essential?

A budget is a financial plan that outlines how you will spend and invest your income over a given period, usually a month. Creating a budget is essential for several reasons:

- **Control**: A budget gives you a clear view of your income and expenses, helping you avoid unnecessary spending and waste.

- **Planning**: With a budget, you can allocate your resources strategically to reach short-, medium-, and long-term goals.

- **Financial Security**: Planning your finances prevents you from falling into debt or facing unpleasant financial surprises. A well-crafted budget ensures you live within your means and helps you build a financial cushion.

- **Peace of Mind**: Knowing exactly where your money is going and how you are managing it provides great mental peace, eliminating financial stress and anxiety.

3.2. Step 1: Identify Your Income

The first step in creating an effective budget is knowing your total income. This includes not only your net salary (what you receive after taxes) but also any other sources of income you might have:

- Additional salaries or bonuses.
- Income from side jobs or freelance work.
- Rental income from properties.
- Returns on investments.
- Any type of regular financial assistance you receive.

It is important to consider only fixed and recurring income, as basing your budget on variable or occasional income can lead to errors or unrealistic expectations. The idea is to have a clear and reliable figure for how much money you have available each month to plan your expenses.

3.3. Step 2: Record Your Expenses

Once you have a clear idea of your income, the next step is to identify and record all your expenses. It is crucial to be meticulous in this step, as small daily expenses can add up to significant amounts at the end of the month.

It is recommended to divide expenses into the following categories:

- **Fixed Expenses**: These are the expenses you must cover month after month, which usually have the same amount. Examples include mortgage or rent, utility bills (electricity, water, internet), insurance, loan payments, and other recurring payments.
- **Variable Expenses**: These are expenses that can fluctuate from one month to the next, such as groceries, transportation, entertainment, and shopping. Although they

are more flexible, it's important to assign a limit to avoid overspending.

- **Occasional Expenses**: This includes expenses that are not monthly but that you know will occur in the future, such as car maintenance, birthday gifts, vacations, etc. The key is to anticipate these expenses and allocate part of your monthly budget for them.

An effective technique to ensure you record all expenses is to keep a daily log for a month. This way, you'll know exactly where every euro is going and be able to detect potential leaks in your finances.

3.4. Step 3: Assign Categories and Set Limits

Once you have a complete list of your expenses, it's time to assign categories and set limits for each of them. This will help ensure that you are allocating your money appropriately to the most important priorities while maintaining balance in your finances.

There are different methods for assigning these categories, but one of the most effective is the 50/30/20 rule:

- **50% for essential needs**: This includes all necessary expenses for your daily life, such as housing, food, transportation, basic utility bills, etc. This percentage is flexible, but the idea is that basic needs should not exceed 50% of your income.

- **30% for wants**: This percentage includes expenses that are not essential but that you enjoy or improve your quality of life, such as dining out, streaming subscriptions, personal shopping, etc. This is the margin you have for some indulgences, as long as you respect the 30% limit.

- **20% for savings and debt repayment**: This is the percentage you will allocate to improve your long-term financial situation. 20% of your income should go toward saving, investing, and paying off debts. This is one of the most important aspects of the budget, as it helps you build an emergency fund, save for major projects, and pay off your debts faster.

This method provides a balance between covering your needs, enjoying certain luxuries, and simultaneously working on your financial future.

3.5. Step 4: Monitor and Adjust Your Budget
A budget is not something you do once and forget about. It's a living tool that should be reviewed and adjusted over time, depending on your needs and changes in your financial situation. Monitoring your budget allows you to:

- Identify areas where you might be overspending.
- See if you are sticking to the limits you set for each category.
- Make adjustments if your income or expenses change unexpectedly.

A good habit is to review your budget at the end of each month. Compare what you planned to spend with what you actually spent, and make adjustments if necessary. For example, if you notice you are spending too much on entertainment, you can reduce that amount for the next month or find ways to cut those costs.

3.6. Tools to Create and Track a Budget
Today, there are many tools and apps that can help you create and track your budget more efficiently. Here are some of the most popular:

- **Custom Spreadsheets**: If you prefer a more personalized approach, Google Sheets or Excel are very useful options for designing your own budget from scratch. You can download templates or create your own, allowing you to tailor them to your specific needs.

- **Budgeting Apps**: Apps like Mint, YNAB (You Need A Budget), Fintonic, or Wallet allow you to connect your bank accounts and automatically categorize your expenses. These apps also send you alerts if you are approaching your budget limits, making it easier to control your spending.

- **Digital Banking**: Many banks offer features to manage your budget directly from their app. These tools often allow you to categorize your expenses, view reports, and adjust your budget based on your financial activity.

3.7. How to Maintain Budget Discipline

Creating a budget is only the first step; the key to success is maintaining the discipline to follow it. Here are some tips to help you stay on track:

- **Automate your savings**: Set up automatic transfers from your checking account to your savings account right after you receive your salary. This way, you'll avoid the temptation to spend that money.

- **Reward yourself for sticking to your budget**: Giving yourself small rewards for staying within your budget can be extra motivation to keep going. For example, if you meet your savings goals for three months, treat yourself to a small luxury.

- **Avoid unnecessary expenses**: Before making a purchase, ask yourself if you really need the item or if it's just a momentary desire. Sometimes delaying a purchase for a few days can help you make a better decision.

- **Be flexible**: Despite the importance of discipline, it's also essential to be flexible. If you have unexpected expenses one month or your income changes, adjust your budget to adapt to the new reality. The key is not to get discouraged and keep moving toward your goals.

3.8. Regular Reviews and Long-Term Adjustments

Over time, your needs, goals, and income may change. Therefore, it is essential to conduct regular reviews of your budget and make long-term adjustments. At least every six months, review your financial priorities and adjust your plan as needed. If your income increases, allocate that extra money to your savings or investment goals before unnecessarily raising your spending.

Chapter 4: Eliminate Debt Smartly

Strategies to Get Out of Debt Without Extreme Sacrifices

Debt is one of the primary financial concerns for many people, and it's not hard to see why. Debts can cause a significant emotional burden, leading to stress, anxiety, and, in some cases, difficulty meeting basic needs. However, getting out of debt doesn't have to be a painful process filled with extreme sacrifices. In this chapter, I will guide you through various practical strategies to eliminate your debts intelligently, without depriving yourself of life's essentials.

4.1. Understand the Nature of Your Debts

Before developing a plan to eliminate your debts, it's crucial to first understand exactly what you are facing. Not all debts are the same, and effectively managing them requires a detailed analysis. Start by making a clear and organized list of all your debts, noting the following:

- The total amount owed.
- The applied interest rate.
- The required minimum monthly payment.
- The repayment term.

Classifying your debts according to these factors will help you prioritize which to pay off first and provide a clearer picture of your financial situation. In general, debts with higher interest rates should be a priority, as they accumulate interest the fastest and can become more challenging to manage over time.

4.2. Snowball vs. Avalanche Strategy

There are two popular and effective methods for eliminating debt: the snowball strategy and the avalanche strategy. Both approaches are useful, but the one you choose will depend on your personal situation and how you prefer to tackle the problem.

- **Snowball Strategy**: With this method, you begin by paying off your smallest debts first, regardless of the interest rate. The idea behind this strategy is to gain motivation by quickly eliminating some debts. As you pay off smaller debts, you free up money to put toward larger debts, creating a "snowball" effect. The psychological boost you get from eliminating smaller debts can give you the confidence and motivation to keep going.

- **Avalanche Strategy**: This method focuses on paying off the debts with the highest interest rate first, which can be more financially efficient in the long run. Although you won't see immediate results like with the snowball method, you will save more money on interest over time. This strategy is ideal if you are focused on maximizing savings and reducing the total time it takes to get out of debt.

Both strategies are valid, and choosing one or the other depends on what best suits your personality and financial needs. Some people prefer to see quick progress, while others feel more comfortable optimizing interest savings.

4.3. Debt Consolidation: Is It a Good Option?

Debt consolidation can be an option that simplifies the debt repayment process, especially if you have multiple sources of debt with different interest rates. Consolidating your debts means combining several debts into one loan with a lower interest rate and a single monthly payment.

Advantages of debt consolidation include:

- **Ease of management**: Instead of making multiple monthly payments to different creditors, you will only have to make one payment.

- **Lower interest rate**: If you can secure a lower interest rate by consolidating your debts, you will save money on interest over the long term.

- **Extended repayment terms**: Depending on the type of consolidation, you may be able to extend the repayment period, which will lower your monthly payment but may increase the overall cost of the debt.

However, it's important to note that consolidation is not a solution for everyone. Debt consolidation can be a useful option if you can secure a significantly lower interest rate than what you currently have. However, you must be careful not to fall into the trap of accumulating more debt after consolidating. If you don't change the financial habits that led you to debt in the first place, consolidation will only delay the problem.

4.4. Negotiating with Creditors

If you feel overwhelmed by your debts and find it difficult to meet your monthly payments, a smart strategy could be to negotiate with your creditors. Often, creditors prefer to work with you and adjust the payment terms rather than risk you defaulting on the debt entirely.

Here are some negotiation strategies you could consider:

- **Request a lower interest rate**: Explain your situation and ask for a reduction in the interest rate. Sometimes creditors are willing to adjust rates to help you meet payments.

- **Extend the repayment term**: Negotiating an extension in the repayment term can lower your monthly payments, giving you more flexibility in your budget.

- **Offer a settlement payment**: If you have access to a significant sum of money, such as a bonus or savings, you can offer a lump sum to settle part of the debt. Often, creditors will accept a smaller amount in exchange for settling the debt immediately.

Negotiating with creditors may seem intimidating, but remember that they also have an interest in recovering their money. The key is to be honest about your situation and be willing to work together to find a solution that works for both parties.

4.5. Automate Your Payments: Avoid Delays and Penalties

A fundamental aspect of eliminating debt intelligently is avoiding payment delays, as these can result in additional fees and damage your credit score. A simple way to ensure you don't miss any payments is to automate your payments. Most banks and loan services allow you to set up automatic payments from your checking account.

Automating payments not only ensures you pay on time but also eliminates the risk of forgetting or failing to follow through. However, make sure there is always enough balance in your account to cover these automatic payments. A good habit is to set up a low-balance alert in your bank account to avoid overdrafts.

4.6. Increase Your Income: A Proactive Solution

While reducing expenses is an important part of the equation for eliminating debt, you can also address the problem from another angle: increasing your income. Having more money available will allow you to accelerate debt repayment without having to make drastic sacrifices to your lifestyle.

Some ideas to increase your income include:

- **Side jobs or freelance work**: If you have skills you can monetize, consider doing extra work in your spare time.

This can be freelancing, tutoring, selling online, or any other activity that allows you to earn extra money.

- **Sell things you no longer need**: Take advantage of the opportunity to sell items you no longer use, such as clothes, electronics, or furniture. Platforms like Wallapop, eBay, or Facebook Marketplace can be useful for this purpose.

- **Investments**: Although it's not always advisable to invest while in debt, if you have some income that you can put to work (such as savings), you can explore safe investments that generate additional returns.

The goal is for the extra money you generate to go directly toward paying off your debts faster. The more you can allocate to debt repayment, the sooner you will be debt-free.

4.7. The Emotional Snowball Effect: Celebrate Small Wins

A crucial part of the debt elimination process is maintaining motivation. When trying to pay off large sums of money, it's easy to get discouraged if you don't see rapid progress. This is where the concept of celebrating small victories becomes essential.

Each time you eliminate a debt, no matter how small, allow yourself a moment of celebration. Recognizing these achievements, such as paying off a credit card or settling a loan, will give you the emotional boost you need to keep going. Emotional motivation is just as important as financial discipline when it comes to eliminating debt.

4.8. Avoid New Debts: Change Your Financial Habits

Finally, a key aspect of eliminating debt smartly is ensuring you are not accumulating new debts while trying to pay off the existing ones. This is a common mistake that can undo all the effort you've put in so far.

Here are some ways to avoid falling into new debt:

- **Cut back on credit card use**: If you can't pay the balance in full each month, consider stopping the use of your credit cards. Opt for using cash or a debit card to better control your spending.

- **Create an emergency fund**: Having an emergency fund will allow you to cover unexpected expenses without resorting to debt.

- **Plan big purchases in advance**: If you know you will need to make a significant purchase (such as an appliance or vacation), start saving for it instead of financing it with debt.

Changing your financial habits is key to ensuring that you not only eliminate your current debts but also stay free from them in the future.

Getting out of debt doesn't have to be a painful process full of extreme sacrifices. With smart strategies like the snowball or avalanche method, debt consolidation, negotiating with creditors, and automating payments, you can begin reducing your debts effectively. Increasing your income and avoiding new debt will help speed up the process. The goal is not only to become debt-free but also to change your financial habits to prevent falling back into debt again.

Chapter 5: Saving: The Key to Financial Well-Being

Simple Techniques to Save Effortlessly

Saving is one of the most important practices for ensuring long-term financial well-being. However, for many people, saving seems like a difficult, and sometimes impossible, task. The good news is that saving doesn't have to be complicated or require major sacrifices. By implementing some simple techniques and practical strategies, it's possible to incorporate saving into your daily life without hardly noticing it. In this chapter, you will learn how to start saving effectively, with little effort and without compromising your quality of life.

5.1. Why Is Saving Crucial?

Before diving into the techniques for saving, it's important to understand why saving is essential for your financial well-being. Saving isn't just a preventive measure for emergencies; it's also a way to build a more secure financial future and achieve your long-term goals. Some of the main reasons to develop the habit of saving include:

- **Creating an emergency fund**: Life is full of unexpected events. Whether it's a car breakdown, a health issue, or an urgent home repair, an emergency fund allows you to handle these situations without turning to debt.
- **Achieving financial goals**: Whether it's buying a house, funding a business, or even planning a vacation, saving is the first step toward achieving any financial goal.

- **Preparing for retirement**: Saving for retirement is essential to ensure you can maintain your standard of living once you stop working.

- **Reducing financial stress**: Having a financial cushion provides peace of mind and a sense of control over your future.

Once you understand the importance of saving, it becomes easier to commit to making it a part of your financial routine.

5.2. Automate Your Savings: Save Without Noticing

One of the most effective methods for saving effortlessly is automating your savings. This approach involves setting up automatic transfers from your checking account to your savings account each month, right after you receive your salary.

The principle behind this technique is simple: if you don't see the money, you won't be tempted to spend it. By automating the process, you make saving a priority, not an option. Many banks offer services that allow you to schedule these automatic transfers, making the process much easier.

The key is to start with an amount you feel comfortable separating from your monthly budget. Even if you can only set aside 5% or 10% of your income, over time, this money will accumulate and provide you with significant savings.

5.3. Adopt the 24-Hour Rule

A simple but effective technique to reduce impulsive spending and increase your savings is to apply the 24-hour rule. This rule states that before making an unplanned purchase, you must wait at least 24 hours to evaluate whether you really need it.

This brief waiting period allows you to reflect on the purchase and weigh whether it is a necessary expense or just a momentary whim. Often, after 24 hours, you'll realize you don't need the item as much as you thought, and the buying impulse will have passed. This habit can significantly reduce unnecessary expenses, allowing you to allocate more money toward savings.

5.4. Track Your Small Expenses

Often, small daily expenses can quickly add up and consume a considerable part of your income without you realizing it. Purchases like morning coffee, snacks at the store, or even subscriptions to services you don't use frequently may seem insignificant, but over time they represent a substantial amount of money you could be saving.

An effective technique is to keep a detailed record of all your small expenses for a month. This will allow you to see exactly where you could reduce or eliminate expenses. While you don't have to completely deprive yourself of these indulgences, reducing their frequency can help you save significantly without feeling like you're making major sacrifices.

5.5. Use the Envelope System

The envelope system is a classic technique that remains effective for many people looking to improve their savings. This method involves assigning an envelope for each category of expenses (rent, food, entertainment, transportation, etc.) and placing the cash you've budgeted for each category at the beginning of the month.

By paying in cash from these envelopes, you have a visual and tangible control of how much money you have left in each category. Once the money in an envelope runs out, you can't spend any more in that category. This system is especially useful for those who tend to overspend with credit or debit cards.

At the end of the month, any leftover money in the envelopes can be directed straight to your savings. It's an effective way to stay within your budget while generating constant savings.

5.6. Round Up and Save the Difference

Another simple technique for saving effortlessly is to take advantage of banking tools that allow you to round up your purchases to the nearest euro and save the difference in a savings account. For example, if you make a purchase for €12.60, the system automatically rounds the purchase to €13.00 and transfers the remaining €0.40 to your savings account.

This small daily rounding may seem insignificant, but over time, those small amounts add up. Some banking apps and savings applications already offer this feature, making it easier for you to save without even noticing.

5.7. Take Advantage of Discounts and Smart Shopping
Another way to save effortlessly is to take advantage of offers and discounts. However, it's crucial not to fall into the trap of buying something just because it's on sale. The key here is to plan your purchases and take advantage of discounts only on the products or services you were already planning to buy.

Some ways to make smart purchases include:

- **Buy in bulk**: If you have space at home, buying non-perishable items in bulk can help you save in the long run. Items like cleaning supplies, toilet paper, or canned foods are often cheaper in large quantities.

- **Look for coupons or discount codes**: Before making an online purchase, always check if there are coupons or discount codes available. There are various websites and apps that help you find discounts for specific stores.

- **Shop during sales seasons**: Taking advantage of sales periods, such as end-of-season sales or Black Friday, is an excellent way to save on products you need. Planning is key to avoiding impulsive purchases and overspending.

5.8. Reduce Your Monthly Bills
One of the most effective ways to increase your savings is by reducing your monthly bills. Here are some ideas for doing so:

- **Review your subscriptions**: Many people pay for streaming services, magazines, or apps they don't frequently use. Review all your subscriptions and cancel those that aren't essential.

- **Negotiate with service providers**: Often, you can save money simply by calling your service providers, like internet or mobile phone companies, and asking for a rate reduction or a cheaper plan. Many companies are willing to offer discounts or promotions to retain customers.

- **Save on energy**: Reducing energy consumption not only benefits the environment but also your wallet. Simple changes like turning off lights when not needed, unplugging appliances when not in use, or investing in energy-efficient bulbs can save money. You can also look for cheaper energy plans with your provider.

5.9. Eliminate Unnecessary Expenses Consciously

A crucial aspect of saving effortlessly is periodically reviewing your expenses and eliminating those that aren't necessary. This is an exercise in becoming aware of where your money is going and which expenses you could reduce or eliminate without affecting your well-being.

Some examples of expenses you might reconsider are:

- Frequent dining out.
- Purchases of unnecessary luxury items.
- Expenses related to unhealthy habits, such as smoking or excessive alcohol consumption.

By reducing or eliminating these expenses, you'll be able to direct that money to your savings account without feeling like you're making major sacrifices.

5.10. Celebrate Your Savings Milestones

Finally, it's important to celebrate your savings achievements. Saving consistently is a habit that requires discipline and commitment, and recognizing your progress is essential for maintaining motivation.

Each time you reach a savings goal, whether big or small, take a moment to celebrate. You can treat yourself to a small indulgence or simply enjoy the satisfaction of knowing you're one step closer to your financial goals.

Saving is the foundation for a stable and prosperous financial future. By applying these simple and practical techniques, such as automating savings, eliminating unnecessary expenses, and using smart tools, you can start saving effortlessly without compromising your quality of life. The goal is to gradually and consistently incorporate saving into your daily routine until it becomes a natural habit.

Chapter 6: Multiply Your Income with New Opportunities

Additional Income Sources to Improve Your Finances

One of the most effective strategies to improve your financial situation and accelerate your economic goals is to increase your income. While controlling and reducing expenses is essential, there comes a point where cutting more is neither viable nor desirable. Instead of focusing exclusively on saving, a powerful way to improve your finances is to explore new opportunities that allow you to multiply your sources of income. In this chapter, you will discover how to leverage your skills, knowledge, and resources to generate additional income, from traditional to more innovative options.

6.1. The Importance of Diversifying Your Income Sources

Relying solely on one source of income, like a salary, can be a risky strategy, as it leaves you vulnerable to unexpected situations like job loss, salary cuts, or labor market changes. Diversifying your income sources not only provides you with greater financial security but also helps you achieve your economic goals faster.

Having multiple income streams allows you to:

- **Increase your financial resilience:** If one income source fails, you still have others to maintain your economic stability.
- **Accelerate debt repayment**: With more available money, you can allocate more to reducing your debts.

- **Achieve long-term goals**: Whether saving for retirement, buying a home, or funding a business, having multiple income sources will help you accumulate money faster.

Now that you understand the importance of diversifying your income, let's explore some additional sources you can take advantage of to improve your financial situation.

6.2. Freelance Work: Capitalize on Your Skills

Freelance work is an excellent option for generating additional income without committing to a full-time job. If you have skills in areas such as writing, graphic design, marketing, translation, programming, or consulting, you can offer your services independently.

Freelance work offers several advantages:

- **Flexible hours**: You can work in your free time, adapting the work hours to your availability.

- **Variety of projects**: Freelance work allows you to participate in diverse projects, which can be an opportunity to develop new skills or explore different interests.

- **Scalable income**: As you gain more clients and experience, you can increase your rates and earn more money.

To start in the freelance world, platforms like Upwork, Fiverr, Freelancer, or even professional networks like LinkedIn allow you to create a profile, showcase your portfolio, and start looking for opportunities.

6.3. Selling Products Online: Become an Entrepreneur

E-commerce has experienced a boom in recent years and is an excellent way to generate additional income. Selling products online does not require a large initial investment, and you can start small and gradually expand.

There are several options for selling products online:

- **Selling your own products**: If you have the skills to create products like clothing, crafts, beauty products, or food, you can sell your creations through platforms like Etsy or on your own online store.

- **Dropshipping**: If you don't have your own product, dropshipping is a viable option. This business model involves selling third-party products without having to manage inventory. You can create an online store and work with suppliers who handle product shipping directly to customers.

- **Reselling products**: Another option is to buy products wholesale or second-hand and resell them through platforms like eBay, Wallapop, or Amazon. This is ideal for people who enjoy finding good deals or unique items.

The key to success in online selling is finding a niche market and offering products that stand out for their quality or uniqueness. Additionally, it's important to develop an effective marketing strategy to attract more customers.

6.4. Monetize Your Hobbies

One of the most satisfying ways to generate additional income is to monetize your hobbies. What you do in your free time can become a source of income if approached strategically.

Some examples of how to turn a hobby into a source of income include:

- **Photography**: If you love photography, you can sell your photos on stock image websites like Shutterstock or Adobe Stock. You can also offer photography services for events, family sessions, or portraits.

- **Creative writing**: If you enjoy writing, consider starting a blog, writing e-books, or working as a freelance writer. Platforms like Amazon KDP allow authors to self-publish their books and earn royalties on each sale.

- **Handicrafts and art**: If you're skilled at making crafts, jewelry, paintings, or any type of art, you can sell your creations online through platforms like Etsy or at local craft fairs.

- **Baking or cooking**: If you enjoy cooking or baking, consider offering your products to friends, family, or neighbors. You can also sell them through social media or home-cooking platforms.

Monetizing your hobbies not only allows you to earn extra money but also enjoy doing something you're passionate about.

6.5. Investments: Make Your Money Work for You

One of the most effective ways to generate additional income in the long term is to invest your money. Although investments require a better understanding of the market and a long-term approach, they are a powerful tool for growing your income without needing to put in extra time.

There are various forms of investment, depending on your risk tolerance and financial goals:

- **Stocks and bonds**: Investing in the stock market can be a profitable way to grow your money over time. You can buy shares in companies or bonds that generate dividends or interest.

- **Mutual funds or ETFs**: If you don't have much investment experience, mutual funds or ETFs (exchange-traded funds) are options that allow you to diversify your portfolio without needing to manage investments actively.

- **Real estate**: If you have available capital, investing in rental properties can be a steady source of passive income. Although it involves a significant initial investment, real estate is often a safe long-term option.

- **Cryptocurrency investments**: If you're interested in the tech world and calculated risks, cryptocurrencies like Bitcoin or Ethereum can offer investment opportunities. However, keep in mind that this market is volatile and not without risks.

Before investing, it's crucial to research and fully understand what you're investing in. If you're unsure where to start, consult a financial advisor to guide you through your first investments.

6.6. Affiliate Programs: Earn Commissions by Promoting Products

Affiliate programs are an excellent way to generate additional income without having to create your own products. Through these programs, you can earn a commission for every sale or action that takes place via the affiliate links you share.

Some platforms offering affiliate programs include Amazon, ClickBank, and many online stores that seek to promote their products through influencers or content creators.

How does it work?

- You sign up for an affiliate program and get a unique link.
- You promote products or services on your blog, social media, or YouTube channel.
- Every time someone makes a purchase through your link, you earn a commission.

Affiliate marketing is a source of passive income because, once you share the link, you can continue generating commissions with little additional effort. The trick is to choose products that truly interest your audience and promote them genuinely.

6.7. Renting Out Assets: Make Money from What You Already Own

Another source of additional income that many people overlook is renting out assets they already own. If you have items you don't use full-time, you can rent them out to generate extra income.

Some ideas include:

- **Renting out rooms or properties**: If you have a spare room at home or a vacant property, consider renting it out through platforms like Airbnb or Booking.

- **Car rental**: If you don't use your car every day, you can rent it to others through platforms like Getaround or Turo.

- **Renting out equipment or tools**: If you own specialized tools, high-quality cameras, or even bicycles, you can rent them to people who need these items temporarily.

This type of income can be an easy way to monetize assets you already have, without needing to make a significant initial investment.

6.8. Create Digital Content: YouTube, Blogs, and Online Courses

In the digital era, content is a powerful tool for generating income. Platforms like YouTube, blogs, and online courses offer multiple opportunities to monetize your knowledge or passion.

- **YouTube**: If you enjoy creating videos, you can generate income through advertising on YouTube, as well as through sponsorships and audience donations.

- **Blogs**: Creating a blog about a topic you're passionate about can be an excellent source of income, whether through advertising, affiliate marketing, or selling your own products.

- **Online courses**: If you have specialized knowledge in a particular area, you can create an online course and sell it through platforms like Udemy or Teachable. Courses are an excellent source of passive income because, once created, they can continue generating income without extra effort.

6.9. Mentoring or Consulting: Share Your Experience

If you have experience in a specific field, you can offer mentoring or consulting services to other people or businesses. Consulting can be offered in areas like business, marketing, finance, personal development, or any other area where you have specialized knowledge.

This type of service is often well-paid, especially if you have a proven track record of success in the area you offer. You can start by promoting your services through your network, social media, or professional platforms.

6.10. Diversify for Success

When considering multiple income sources, it's important not to try to do everything at once. Choose one or two additional sources that best suit your interests, skills, and situation, and start there. As you become more comfortable and generate more income, you can diversify further.

Remember that generating additional income requires time and effort, but the long-term rewards can be significant. The key is to start gradually, with a clear strategy focused on your long-term financial goals.

Multiplying your income through new opportunities will not only improve your financial situation but also give you a greater sense of control and financial freedom. Exploring freelance work, investing, selling products online, or monetizing your hobbies are just some of the many options available to you. The key is to diversify and take advantage of all the opportunities to grow your finances smartly.

Chapter 7: Basic Investments for Beginner

How to Grow Your Money Safely

When it comes to improving your finances and securing your economic future, investing is one of the most powerful tools at your disposal. While saving is crucial for stability, investments allow your money to grow and work for you, generating returns over time. For many people, the world of investments may seem complex and full of risks, but it doesn't have to be. With the right approach and choosing safe investments, any beginner can start building a profitable investment portfolio.

In this chapter, I will guide you through the basics of investing, safe options to get started, and some key tips to help you make informed decisions and grow your money safely.

7.1. What is an Investment?

An investment is the act of allocating a sum of money to an asset with the expectation that its value will increase over time or that it will generate a return, either in the form of interest, dividends, or capital appreciation. The main difference between saving and investing is that with investing, you take on some risk in search of a higher reward, whereas saving typically involves keeping your money in a safe place without significant growth.

The goal of investing is to make your money work for you, allowing you to generate passive income or increase your wealth in the long term.

7.2. The Importance of Starting to Invest Early

One of the most important principles of investing is to start as early as possible. This is due to the effect of compound interest, which allows your gains to generate more gains over time. The longer you keep your money invested, the greater the benefits you will obtain.

For example, if you start investing at age 25 and continue until age 65, even with small regular contributions, you are likely to accumulate a significant amount of money thanks to compound interest. On the other hand, if you wait until you're 35 or 40 to start investing, your investments will have less time to grow and generate returns.

7.3. Assess Your Risk Tolerance

Before you start investing, it's crucial to assess your risk tolerance. Risk is the possibility that you could lose part or all of the money you've invested, and all investments carry a certain degree of risk. However, not all investors have the same tolerance for risk. Some people prefer safer options with modest returns, while others are willing to take on more risk in search of higher rewards.

Your risk tolerance depends on several factors, such as:

- **Age**: Younger investors tend to have a higher tolerance for risk because they have more time to recover from potential losses.

- **Financial goals**: If your goal is to save for retirement in several decades, you might be willing to take on more risk than if you need the money in the next five years.

- **Financial situation**: People with a larger financial cushion can afford to take greater risks, while those who rely on every euro they invest might prefer safer options.

7.4. Types of Investments for Beginners

There are several types of investments suitable for beginners. Below are some of the most common and safest options to start growing your money.

7.4.1. High-Yield Savings Accounts

Although technically not an investment, high-yield savings accounts are an ideal option for those looking for a safe place to store their money while earning interest. These accounts offer higher interest rates than traditional savings accounts, allowing you to earn more on your money without taking on virtually any risk.

High-yield savings accounts are perfect for those just starting and wanting to earn a bit more than a regular bank account would offer. However, the returns are generally modest compared to other investments.

7.4.2. Bonds

Bonds are a relatively safe form of investment where you lend money to a company or government in exchange for receiving periodic interest payments and the return of the original amount (principal) at the end of a specified period.

There are different types of bonds, including:

- **Government bonds**: These are issued by national governments and are considered one of the safest investments, as governments generally fulfill their payments. In countries like Spain, government bonds are a popular option.
- **Corporate bonds**: These are issued by companies to fund projects or expansion. Corporate bonds usually offer higher interest rates than government bonds but also carry more risk.

Bonds are an excellent option for those seeking stable, reliable income, especially compared to riskier investments like stocks.

7.4.3. Stocks

Stocks represent partial ownership in a company. When you buy stocks, you become a shareholder and can benefit if the company grows and its stock price increases. Additionally, many companies pay dividends to their shareholders, meaning you will receive a portion of the company's profits periodically.

Although investing in stocks can offer high returns in the long term, it also carries greater risk, as stock prices can fluctuate significantly in the short term. However, stocks are an excellent option for long-term investors who are willing to endure some volatility in search of higher rewards.

7.4.4. Mutual Funds

Mutual funds are an excellent option for beginners who want to diversify their investments without having to manage a portfolio of individual stocks or bonds. In a mutual fund, your money is pooled with other investors' money and used to purchase a wide variety of assets, which helps reduce risk.

There are several types of mutual funds:

- **Stock funds**: These funds invest primarily in stocks and offer the potential for high returns, though with higher risk.

- **Bond funds**: These funds invest in bonds and are typically more stable than stock funds.

- **Index funds**: These are particularly popular for beginner investors. An index fund tracks a market index, such as the S&P 500, meaning you invest in a broad set of companies without having to select individual stocks.

Mutual funds offer excellent diversification and are often managed by professionals, making them an attractive option for beginners looking to invest without doing extensive research on their own.

7.4.5. ETFs (Exchange-Traded Funds)

ETFs are similar to mutual funds in that they invest in a basket of assets, but they are traded on the stock market like individual stocks. This means you can buy and sell ETFs at any time during market hours.

ETFs are an excellent option for beginners because they offer diversification, lower fees than traditional mutual funds, and the flexibility to trade in real-time. Many ETFs track market indices, making them a low-risk and affordable investment option to start with.

7.5. The Rule of Diversification: Don't Put All Your Eggs in One Basket

One of the most important rules of investing is diversification, which means not putting all your money into a single type of investment. By diversifying, you reduce the risk of a bad investment significantly impacting your portfolio.

A diversified portfolio will include a mix of different asset types, such as stocks, bonds, real estate, and cash. This mix will protect you in case one asset class underperforms, as other assets may offset those losses.

Diversification is especially important for beginners, as it minimizes risk and increases the stability of your investment portfolio over time.

7.6. Invest Consistently: The Power of Dollar-Cost Averaging

A simple and effective technique for beginner investors is the dollar-cost averaging strategy, which involves investing the same amount of money at regular intervals, regardless of market fluctuations. This could be done monthly or quarterly, for example.

Dollar-cost averaging allows you to buy more shares when prices are low and fewer when prices are high, reducing the impact of market volatility on your portfolio. Additionally, investing consistently creates a positive habit of saving and investing, making it easier for your money to grow over time.

7.7. Avoid Market Timing

One of the most common mistakes beginner investors make is trying to "time the market," meaning they attempt to buy and sell assets at the perfect moment to maximize gains. This approach is extremely difficult to execute successfully, even for professional investors.

Instead of trying to predict the market's ups and downs, focus on long-term investing and remain calm during market downturns. Patience is key, as markets tend to recover over time, and those who stay invested usually reap greater benefits in the long run.

7.8. Tips for Beginners: Growing Your Money Safely

To grow your money safely as a beginner, here are some additional tips:

- **Start small**: You don't need large sums of money to start investing. Begin with what you can and increase your investments as you become more comfortable.

- **Educate yourself and stay informed**: Learn about the different types of investments and continue educating yourself as you progress. There are numerous online resources, books, and courses that can help you improve your investment skills.

- **Have a long-term vision**: Investing is a marathon, not a sprint. Keep a long-term perspective and don't get caught up in daily market fluctuations.

- **Consult a financial advisor**: If you feel uncertain or don't know where to start, consider consulting a financial advisor. A professional can help you develop an investment strategy tailored to your goals and risk tolerance.

Investing isn't just for financial experts. Anyone can start growing their money safely with a strategic and informed approach. Whether you choose bonds, stocks, mutual funds, or ETFs, the important thing is to diversify, invest consistently, and keep a long-term vision. As you develop your investment skills and increase your confidence, you'll see your efforts begin to bear fruit, helping you achieve your financial goals and build a stronger economic future.

Chapter 8: How to Protect Your Finances from the Unexpected

Planning for Unforeseen Events

Life is full of surprises, from last-minute home repairs to medical emergencies or job loss. These unexpected events can significantly affect your financial stability if you're not prepared. Proper planning allows you to face these challenges with confidence and avoid falling into debt or making rushed financial decisions. In this chapter, we will explore the most effective strategies to protect your finances from the unexpected, ensuring that your financial future doesn't depend on chance.

8.1. The Importance of Being Prepared

No one can predict the future, but what we can do is prepare for the unexpected. Unforeseen events tend to happen when we least expect them, and they can test our ability to respond both emotionally and financially. Being prepared not only gives you peace of mind but also helps you avoid making hasty decisions that could harm your long-term finances.

The most common unexpected events that can affect your finances include:

- Medical or health emergencies.
- Job loss or income reduction.
- Unplanned home or vehicle repairs.
- Expenses due to natural disasters or theft.

Having a financial plan for these events will help minimize their impact and allow you to recover quickly without compromising your economic stability.

8.2. Emergency Fund: Your First Line of Defense

The emergency fund is the most powerful tool you can have to protect your finances from the unexpected. This fund is a cushion of money set aside exclusively to cover unforeseen expenses and should be easily accessible at any time.

How much money do you need in your emergency fund?

The ideal amount for your emergency fund depends on your financial and personal situation. However, a general recommendation is to have at least three to six months of essential expenses covered. This includes basic expenses like housing, food, transportation, and insurance. If you have variable income or rely on a single salary, it's advisable to have a more robust emergency fund, covering at least six months of expenses.

Where to keep your emergency fund?

The emergency fund should be in an account that is easily accessible, but at the same time provides some return. Some options include:

- **High-yield savings accounts**: These offer higher interest rates than traditional savings accounts and are liquid, meaning you can withdraw the money when needed.

- **Short-term certificates of deposit (CDs)**: If you prefer not to keep all your fund in a savings account, short-term CDs can offer a higher return, though with a penalty for early withdrawals.

The most important thing is that this fund is kept separate from your checking accounts and used exclusively for emergencies, avoiding the temptation to use it for everyday expenses.

8.3. Insurance: A Protective Shield for Your Finances

Insurance is another essential tool to protect your finances from unexpected events. Insurance helps cover unforeseen expenses that could devastate your finances, such as accidents, natural disasters, medical emergencies, or the death of the primary breadwinner.

Essential types of insurance

- **Health insurance**: Medical expenses can be devastating if you don't have good health insurance. This type of insurance is crucial for covering hospital costs, medical treatments, medications, and other health-related needs.

- **Life insurance**: Life insurance is especially important if you have dependents who rely on your income. In the event of death, this insurance provides a payout to your beneficiaries, helping them cover expenses and maintain their lifestyle.

- **Unemployment or disability insurance**: This type of insurance protects you if you lose your job or if you suffer a disability that prevents you from working. It provides income for a determined period, giving you time to recover or find new employment without your finances being immediately affected.

- **Home and auto insurance**: These insurances protect your physical assets, such as your home and car, in case of damage, theft, or accidents. Having good home or auto insurance coverage helps you avoid significant unexpected expenses in the event of unforeseen circumstances.

When choosing insurance, make sure to review the policy's coverage and limits to ensure they suit your needs and adequately protect you in the event of an unexpected event.

8.4. Diversifying Income: Minimize Risks

As mentioned in previous chapters, one of the best ways to protect your finances is by diversifying your income sources. If you rely solely on one job or income source, you are more vulnerable to economic surprises, such as job loss or reduced work hours.

Diversifying income can include:

- Additional income through freelance work or self-employment projects.
- Investing in real estate to generate passive income.
- Running a side business or generating income online.

Having more than one source of income gives you greater financial security because if one fails, you will still have others to maintain your economic stability.

8.5. Long-Term Financial Planning

Long-term financial planning is essential to be prepared for the unexpected. This planning includes not only saving and investing but also creating a comprehensive plan that allows you to cover different scenarios.

Key elements of long-term financial planning include:

- **Saving for retirement**: Ensure that you are regularly contributing to your pension plan or retirement accounts. The earlier you start, the better prepared you will be for unforeseen events during old age.
- **Diversified investments**: Having a well-diversified investment portfolio will protect you against market fluctuations and help grow your money safely.
- **Debt management**: Minimizing or eliminating your debts entirely will give you more financial flexibility in the event of an unexpected event. If you are debt-free, your monthly

obligations will be lower, making it easier to deal with emergencies.

8.6. Controlling Expenses and a Flexible Budget

One of the most important aspects of protecting your finances from the unexpected is having a flexible budget that allows you to adjust your expenses according to circumstances. A flexible budget allows you to adapt to changes without needing to resort to debt or compromising your financial stability.

Some tips for maintaining a flexible budget include:

- **Review and adjust your budget regularly**: If you experience a change in income or face an unexpected event, review your budget and adjust your spending categories accordingly.

- **Create an emergency spending plan**: Define which expenses you can reduce or eliminate in the event of a financial emergency. This could include reducing entertainment, postponing major purchases, or cutting variable expenses.

- **Avoid lifestyle inflation with new income**: When your income increases, it can be tempting to raise your spending as well. Instead, allocate a significant portion of that additional income to your emergency fund or investments, giving you greater financial security.

8.7. The Importance of Having a Will and Succession Plan

Although we often don't think about it, having a will and a succession plan is an essential part of financial protection. A will ensures that your assets are distributed according to your wishes in the event of death, which can help your loved ones avoid legal complications or family disputes. A good succession plan will also help minimize the taxes your heirs may face, allowing them to access your assets more quickly and efficiently.

In addition to a will, it's also advisable to consider other forms of estate planning, such as creating trusts or designating beneficiaries on your financial accounts.

8.8. Keep Your Financial Education Active

Finally, one of the best ways to protect your finances from the unexpected is to stay financially educated. Knowledge is a powerful tool for making sound decisions and avoiding panic when unforeseen situations arise. Stay up to date on best practices for financial management, investing, and planning to ensure you are well prepared for any eventuality.

Some ways to keep your financial education active include:

- Reading books and blogs on personal finance.
- Taking online courses on investing or financial planning.
- Regularly consulting with a financial advisor to review your plans and adjust them as necessary.

Protecting your finances from the unexpected isn't just a matter of luck; it's about being well-prepared and taking proactive measures. By building an emergency fund, having the right insurance, diversifying your income, and creating a solid financial plan, you'll be in a much stronger position to face any challenges life throws at you. The key is to plan ahead and be willing to adapt to circumstances, ensuring that your financial stability remains intact even in times of uncertainty.

Chapter 9: Living Within Your Means

Controlling Expenses Without Sacrificing Quality of Life

Living within your means is one of the fundamental keys to achieving financial stability and maintaining control over your finances. However, many people associate this concept with sacrifice, extreme austerity, or giving up enjoying life. In reality, living within your means doesn't mean depriving yourself of everything you like; instead, it's about managing your income and expenses wisely, to maintain a financial balance that allows you to enjoy a good quality of life without going into debt or compromising your economic future.

In this chapter, we will explore strategies to control your expenses without sacrificing your well-being, providing you with practical tools to manage your money effectively, save, and still live a fulfilling and satisfying life.

9.1. Understand Your Real Capabilities

The first step to living within your means is to understand exactly what those means are. Often, financial mismanagement arises when we don't have a clear view of our income and expenses, which can lead to spending more than we can really afford. To avoid this problem, it's important to conduct a financial assessment that includes:

- **Net income**: The amount of money you receive each month after taxes and deductions. This is the amount you can actually use to cover your expenses and save.

- **Essential expenses**: The expenses you need to cover to maintain your daily life, such as housing, food, transportation, utilities, and insurance. These are unavoidable expenses and should be prioritized in your budget.

- **Discretionary expenses**: These are the expenses that are not essential but bring satisfaction and improve your quality of life, such as dining out, entertainment, clothing, travel, etc. Although they are important, this is where you can adjust or cut back if necessary.

Once you have a clear overview of your income and expenses, you can start planning how to allocate your resources efficiently, ensuring that you are not spending more than you earn.

9.2. The 50/30/20 Rule: A Balanced Approach to Controlling Expenses

One of the most popular formulas for living within your means without sacrificing your quality of life is the 50/30/20 rule, which helps you organize your finances in a balanced way. This rule suggests dividing your net income into three main categories:

- **50% for basic needs**: This category includes everything you need to live, such as rent or mortgage, basic utility bills, transportation, food, and insurance. The idea is not to spend more than 50% of your income on these essential expenses.

- **30% for wants or discretionary spending**: This category covers non-essential expenses that contribute to your well-being, such as dining out, entertainment, clothing, travel, hobbies, etc. Here you can enjoy life without feeling guilty, as long as it doesn't exceed 30% of your income.

- **20% for savings and debt**: The remaining 20% of your income should be allocated to your long-term financial goals, such as savings, investments, or debt repayment. This percentage helps you build a solid financial foundation for the future and avoid relying on loans or credit cards.

Applying this rule allows you to maintain a balance between covering your needs, enjoying life, and, at the same time, progressing towards financial stability.

9.3. Control Emotional Spending

Emotional spending is one of the biggest enemies of financial stability. Often, we buy things on impulse as a way to cope with stress, sadness, or dissatisfaction, which leads us to spend more than necessary. This type of spending can be dangerous as it can quickly disrupt your finances without you realizing it.

To avoid emotional spending, it's useful to follow some steps:

- **Recognize your emotional patterns**: Take note of when and why you feel tempted to spend. Do you tend to shop when you're stressed or bored? Identifying these moments will help you make more conscious decisions.

- **Implement the 24-hour rule**: Before making an impulse purchase, wait 24 hours. This time will allow you to reflect on whether you really need the item or if it's just an impulsive purchase.

- **Find alternatives**: If you tend to spend to cope with your emotions, look for alternatives that don't affect your wallet, such as exercising, meditating, or talking to a friend. These activities can help you manage stress without resorting to spending.

9.4. Eliminate or Reduce Unnecessary Expenses

One of the most effective ways to live within your means is to identify and eliminate unnecessary expenses. Often, we spend money on things we don't need or use, which can significantly impact our finances over time.

Here are some strategies to reduce expenses without affecting your quality of life:

- **Review your subscriptions**: Many people have subscriptions they don't use, such as streaming services, gym memberships, or digital magazines. Review all your subscriptions and cancel those you don't use frequently.

- **Shop with a list**: When you go shopping, bring a list and stick to it. This will help you avoid impulse purchases and focus on what you really need.

- **Compare prices**: Before making a major purchase, compare prices at different stores or online. Often, you can find the same product at a lower price, allowing you to save without sacrificing quality.

- **Make smart purchases**: Take advantage of sales seasons, use discount coupons, and buy non-perishable items in bulk that you use frequently. These small actions can add up to significant savings over time.

9.5. Live Without Consumer Debt

One of the biggest financial traps is relying on consumer debt, such as credit cards or personal loans, to fund your daily expenses. While credit cards can be useful in certain situations, living on credit can quickly lead you to accumulate debts that are difficult to pay off.

To avoid falling into this trap, follow these tips:

- **Use credit cards responsibly**: If you use a credit card, make sure to pay off the full balance each month to avoid interest. If you can't do this, reduce its use until you can pay off the balance.

- **Avoid financing discretionary purchases**: Don't use credit to finance non-essential expenses like clothing, entertainment, or travel. If you can't pay for something in cash, consider whether you really need it.

- **Set up an emergency fund**: Having an emergency fund allows you to cover unexpected expenses without having to rely on credit cards or personal loans. This protects you from falling into debt when an unforeseen event occurs.

9.6. Learn to Prioritize Your Spending

To live within your means without sacrificing your quality of life, it's essential to prioritize your spending. This means deciding in which areas you want to spend more and where you can save. Not all expenses have the same value to you, and it's important to identify which ones are most important and where you can cut back without affecting your well-being.

- **Spend on what brings you satisfaction**: If there's something you really enjoy, such as traveling or enjoying good food, it's okay to spend on it as long as it's within your budget. The trick is to cut back in other, less important areas.

- **Avoid spending due to social pressure**: Don't feel obliged to spend money on things just because other people do. Whether it's branded clothing, expensive dinners, or the latest tech gadgets, make sure every purchase aligns with your priorities, not others' expectations.

9.7. Save Instead of Overspending

One of the most powerful strategies for living within your means is to make saving a priority rather than spending all your money on unnecessary things. Every time you receive money, whether it's your salary, a bonus, or additional income, set aside a portion for savings before allocating the rest to expenses.

A useful technique is the "pay yourself first" strategy. This means that before paying your bills or covering daily expenses, you set aside a percentage of your income for savings. This way, you are always contributing to your future financial well-being without feeling like you are sacrificing your current needs.

9.8. Maximize Your Quality of Life Without Spending More

Finally, it's important to remember that you don't always need to spend money to improve your quality of life. There are many ways to enjoy a fulfilling life without making big expenditures:

- **Take advantage of free or low-cost activities**: Many cities offer free cultural activities, such as concerts, exhibitions, or classes. You can also enjoy nature, organize outings with friends, or do creative activities without spending much.

- **Invest in experiences, not things**: Numerous studies show that experiences make us happier than material possessions. Instead of spending money on things, invest in experiences that give you lasting memories and satisfaction.

- **Strengthen your relationships**: Interpersonal relationships are one of the greatest contributors to our happiness. Spending time with loved ones doesn't require spending money, and often the best experiences are those shared with others.

Living within your means doesn't mean giving up enjoying life. With a balanced approach, you can control your expenses, prioritize what's most important to you, and, at the same time, progress toward greater financial stability. By learning to manage your resources effectively, reducing unnecessary expenses, and prioritizing savings, you'll be building a stronger economic future without sacrificing your current well-being.

Chapter 10: Continuous Financial Education

The Importance of Continuing to Learn About Finance

Financial education is an ongoing process that doesn't end once you learn to manage a budget or invest your first savings. In a world where the economy, financial markets, and regulations are constantly changing, it's crucial to stay informed and up to date on best financial practices. Those who commit to continuously learning about finance are better prepared to make informed decisions, protect their wealth, and seize new growth opportunities.

In this chapter, we will explore the importance of continuous financial education and how you can integrate it into your life to improve your financial skills, knowledge, and outcomes.

10.1. What is Continuous Financial Education?

Continuous financial education refers to the commitment to regularly learning about how to manage your money, invest, save, and plan for your financial future. No matter what stage of life you are in, there is always more to discover, as the world of personal finance and investments is constantly evolving.

This ongoing learning not only covers the basics of saving or expense management but also more complex topics like tax planning, investment diversification, market fluctuations, or new financial opportunities arising from technology and globalization.

10.2. Why Continuing to Learn About Finance is Essential

One of the biggest mistakes people can make is assuming they already know enough about finance. In reality, staying up to date on financial topics is essential to making the most of your resources and protecting yourself from unnecessary risks. Here are some key reasons to keep learning about finance:

10.2.1. The Financial World is Constantly Changing

Financial markets, tax laws, economic policies, and consumer trends change over time. What was an effective investment strategy 10 years ago may no longer be as relevant today. New financial products, such as cryptocurrencies, index funds, or automated investment platforms, offer new opportunities but also new risks. Staying informed allows you to adapt and take advantage of what the financial environment offers.

10.2.2. Inflation and Money Devaluation

Understanding how inflation affects your purchasing power is essential for long-term financial planning. If you don't adjust your saving and investment strategies to combat the effects of inflation, the money you have today may be worth significantly less in the future. Learning how to protect your assets against inflation will allow you to maintain and grow your wealth over time.

10.2.3. Better Investment Opportunities

Continuous financial education helps you identify better investment opportunities and optimize your portfolio. As you learn more about risk management, diversification, and different asset classes, you can make more informed decisions that maximize your returns and minimize losses. Knowledge about new forms of investment, such as sustainable funds or specialized ETFs, allows you to adapt your portfolio to your interests and needs.

10.2.4. Improved Decision-Making

A person with a solid financial education can make well-informed decisions, reducing the likelihood of falling into financial traps, such as scams, excessive debt, or high-risk investments without adequate understanding. With up-to-date knowledge, you can objectively evaluate the options available, avoid common mistakes, and make decisions that align with your long-term financial goals.

10.2.5. Long-Term Financial Security

Financial security isn't achieved overnight, but with continuous learning and the application of effective strategies, you can ensure that your financial future is well-protected. Financial education allows you to build a plan that includes everything from retirement savings to tax planning, giving you peace of mind and confidence that you are taking the right steps to protect your economic well-being.

10.3. How to Integrate Financial Education Into Your Daily Life

Incorporating financial education into your daily life doesn't have to be overwhelming or time-consuming. There are many practical and accessible ways to keep learning about finance while managing your everyday responsibilities.

10.3.1. Read Books and Financial Articles

One of the most effective ways to stay up to date on financial topics is to read books, blogs, or articles written by experts. Some well-known authors, like Robert Kiyosaki (*Rich Dad, Poor Dad*), Dave Ramsey (*The Total Money Makeover*), or Tony Robbins (*Money: Master the Game*), offer clear and direct insights into how to manage your finances and improve your economic situation.

Additionally, many blogs and websites regularly publish articles on investment, saving, budgeting, and financial planning, such as

NerdWallet, Investopedia, or The Balance. Regularly reading these resources can keep you informed about the latest trends and advice.

10.3.2. Listen to Podcasts or Audiobooks

If you don't have time to read, podcasts and audiobooks are an excellent alternative. There are numerous podcasts dedicated to personal finance, investing, and economic development that you can listen to while driving, exercising, or doing other activities. Some recommended podcasts include *ChooseFI*, *Planet Money*, or *BiggerPockets Money*.

Audiobooks are also a convenient way to learn while you're busy. Many platforms, such as Audible or Google Play, offer a wide selection of titles on personal finance and financial development.

10.3.3. Take Online Courses

Today, there are many online learning platforms offering courses on personal finance, investment, and financial planning. Platforms like Udemy, Coursera, or Khan Academy offer free and paid courses that cover everything from basic concepts to more advanced topics.

Taking an online course allows you to delve into specific subjects and acquire knowledge in a structured manner at your own pace. Some recommended courses include those on debt management, stock market investing, cryptocurrencies, real estate, and retirement planning.

10.3.4. Participate in Forums and Communities

Online forums and communities dedicated to personal finance and investments can be a great source of learning and support. Participating in these communities allows you to share experiences, ask questions, and learn from others with similar interests.

Platforms like Reddit have sub-communities like r/personalfinance or r/investing, where thousands of users discuss financial topics and offer helpful advice. You can also join groups on social media, like

Facebook or LinkedIn, where members share educational content, strategies, and experiences.

10.3.5. Consult a Financial Advisor

Although learning on your own is important, having the support of a professional financial advisor can be very helpful, especially if you have complex questions or need personalized guidance. An advisor can help you plan strategically, adjust your investment portfolio, and provide you with up-to-date information on best financial practices.

Additionally, consulting with an advisor provides an external and objective perspective that helps you avoid common mistakes and make better decisions to achieve your goals.

10.4. Adapt to New Financial Trends and Technologies

In recent years, we have seen the emergence of new financial trends and technologies that are changing the way we manage our money. Continuous financial education allows you to adapt to these changes and take advantage of the opportunities they offer.

10.4.1. Fintech and Digital Tools

Financial technologies (fintech) have revolutionized the way we manage money. Mobile apps for budgeting, automated investments (like robo-advisors), and digital payment platforms are just a few examples of how technology has made financial management easier.

By learning about these new tools, you can find more efficient ways to manage your finances, improve expense control, and invest automatically.

10.4.2. Cryptocurrencies and Blockchain

Cryptocurrencies and blockchain technology have emerged as a disruptive trend in the financial world. Although they are still relatively new and volatile, cryptocurrencies have shown the potential to change the way we conduct transactions and store value.

While investing in cryptocurrencies may not be suitable for everyone, it's important to educate yourself on how they work, their risks, and their possible long-term applications, as they may become an important part of the global financial system in the future.

10.5. Stay Motivated: Financial Education is an Investment in Yourself

The process of learning about finance isn't always easy or fast, but financial education is an investment in yourself. Every new concept you understand, every strategy you apply, and every informed decision you make brings you one step closer to financial security and freedom.

Staying motivated is key to continuing to learn, and one of the greatest incentives is seeing your efforts pay off. As you learn and apply new knowledge, you will see improvements in your ability to save, invest, and make smart financial decisions.

Continuous financial education is essential for maintaining control over your finances, adapting to changes in the financial environment, and taking advantage of new opportunities. Through reading, courses, podcasts, and consulting with experts, you can continue developing your skills and knowledge, allowing you to build a solid and secure financial future. No matter where you are today, there is always more to learn, and the financial knowledge you acquire will open doors to a fuller and more successful economic life.

Chapter 11: The Impact of Taxes on Your Economy

Strategies to Optimize Your Taxes

Taxes are an inevitable reality in everyone's life, and their impact on our personal economy can be significant. Although many people see taxes as an uncontrollable expense, the truth is that there are various strategies you can employ to optimize your tax situation and minimize the negative impact they may have on your finances. Learning how to manage and optimize your taxes will not only help you reduce your tax burden but also allow you to take advantage of tax incentives and maximize your income.

In this chapter, we will explore the importance of understanding how taxes affect your economy, the most effective strategies for optimizing your taxes, and some practical tips for better managing your tax obligations.

11.1. Understanding the Impact of Taxes on Your Personal Finances

The first step in optimizing your taxes is understanding how they influence your personal economy. Taxes directly affect your disposable income, which is the amount of money you have left after taxes are deducted from your salary or earnings. These include income taxes, consumption taxes (such as VAT), wealth taxes, and in some cases, capital gains taxes.

The key to improving your tax situation is maximizing the net income you retain after paying taxes. Through effective tax planning, you can ensure that you pay the appropriate amount and benefit from the tax opportunities available under your country's legislation.

11.2. The Importance of Tax Planning

Tax planning is an essential tool for optimizing your taxes. This involves making financial decisions strategically to legally reduce your tax burden. There are multiple ways to do this, from taking advantage of deductions and tax credits to choosing the right investments or structuring your income more efficiently.

By proactively planning your taxes, you can reduce the amount of money you pay to the government, which in turn allows you to increase your savings, investments, or discretionary spending.

11.3. Strategies to Optimize Your Taxes

There are several strategies you can use to optimize your taxes and reduce the amount you pay each year. Below are some of the most common and effective ones.

11.3.1. Take Advantage of Tax Deductions

Tax deductions are expenses that the government allows you to subtract from your taxable income, reducing the amount on which you pay taxes. Maximizing tax deductions is one of the simplest and most effective ways to reduce your tax burden.

Some common tax deductions include:

- **Medical and health expenses**: In many countries, you can deduct certain medical expenses, such as doctor visits, surgeries, medications, and health insurance premiums, as long as they exceed a specific percentage of your income.
- **Contributions to retirement plans**: Contributions to retirement plans, such as pension plans in Spain or IRAs and 401(k)s in the United States, can be deducted from your income, reducing your taxable base. These contributions not

only save you taxes now but also prepare you for a financially secure future.

- **Charitable donations**: Donations to recognized charitable organizations are often tax-deductible. If you make charitable contributions, be sure to keep receipts to take advantage of these deductions.

- **Mortgage interest**: In many cases, you can deduct the interest you pay on your mortgage. This is an important deduction, especially for those who have recently purchased a home and have a high mortgage interest balance.

11.3.2. Use Tax Credits

Unlike deductions, which reduce your taxable income, tax credits directly reduce the amount of taxes you owe. There are many types of tax credits, and it's essential to know which ones apply to your situation.

Some examples of common tax credits include:

- **Child tax credit**: This credit is awarded to parents with children under a certain age, directly reducing the amount you owe in taxes.

- **Energy-saving credits**: Some governments offer tax credits to those who make energy-efficiency improvements to their home, such as installing solar panels or energy-efficient windows.

- **Education credits**: If you or your dependent are studying, you may have access to tax credits for education-related expenses, such as tuition or study materials.

- **Credits for the elderly or disabled**: In some cases, governments offer specific tax credits for seniors or disabled individuals who meet certain requirements.

Taking advantage of tax credits is key to directly reducing the amount you owe in taxes and can significantly impact your tax situation.

11.3.3. Optimize the Use of Your Investments

A solid investment strategy can also help you optimize your taxes. Below are some ways you can make your investments work in your favor from a tax perspective.

- **Use tax-beneficial investment accounts**: Many investment accounts, such as retirement accounts (Pension Plans or IRAs), are designed to offer tax benefits. Gains within these accounts grow tax-deferred until you withdraw the money. Investing through these accounts can help you defer taxes and, in some cases, avoid them altogether.

- **Capital gains tax management**: Capital gains taxes are the taxes you pay on profits earned from selling an asset (stocks, real estate, etc.). If you hold your investments for a longer period, you may benefit from lower tax rates on long-term capital gains rather than short-term gains. Additionally, you can use capital losses to offset gains and reduce your overall tax bill.

- **Automatic reinvestment and tax deferral**: If you reinvest earnings from an investment instead of withdrawing them, in many cases, you can defer taxes, allowing your investments to continue growing without tax interruptions.

11.3.4. Review Your Tax Situation Annually

Tax legislation changes constantly, and what was effective last year may not be this year. For this reason, it's important to review your tax situation annually. This will ensure that you're taking advantage of all available deductions and tax credits and give you the opportunity to adjust your tax strategy if necessary.

Working with a tax advisor can be an excellent way to stay up to date on changes in tax law and ensure that you're doing everything possible to optimize your taxes.

11.4. The Importance of Good Record-Keeping

One of the keys to making the most of deductions and tax credits is keeping good records of your personal finances. This includes saving receipts, invoices, and other documents related to expenses you may deduct, as well as financial transactions related to investments, donations, and retirement contributions.

Having these documents organized will not only help you optimize your taxes but also make the tax filing process easier each year. Many taxpayers lose out on important deductions simply because they didn't keep the necessary receipts or invoices.

11.5. Avoid Common Tax Planning Mistakes

A lack of planning or knowledge of tax benefits can cause you to pay more taxes than you should. Here are some common mistakes to avoid to ensure that you're correctly optimizing your taxes:

- **Not taking advantage of all available deductions and credits**: Many people are unaware of all the deductions and credits they're eligible for. It's important to research which tax benefits apply to your specific situation.

- **Not reviewing changes in tax legislation**: As mentioned earlier, tax laws change regularly. Failing to stay informed about these changes could mean missing out on optimization opportunities.

- **Not investing in tax-beneficial products**: If you're not taking advantage of investment accounts with tax advantages, such as retirement plans, you could be paying more taxes than necessary. These accounts not only help reduce your taxable income but also prepare you for the future.

11.6. Tools and Resources to Optimize Your Taxes

There are many tools and resources available to help you optimize your taxes and better manage your tax situation. Some options include:

- **Tax filing software**: Platforms like TurboTax, H&R Block, or TaxAct can help you calculate your tax return, guiding you step by step and ensuring that you take advantage of all available deductions and credits.

- **Expense tracking apps**: Apps like Mint, YNAB (You Need A Budget), or Fintonic can help you keep detailed records of your expenses, making it easier to claim tax deductions.

- **Tax consultants**: Working with a tax consultant can be an excellent investment if you have a complex financial situation or want to ensure that you're taking advantage of all possible tax opportunities.

11.7. When is it Time to Consult a Tax Advisor?

While many people can manage their own taxes, there are times when it's advisable to consult a professional tax advisor. Some cases where you might need an advisor include:

- **If you have a complex financial situation**, such as multiple income sources, foreign investments, or properties.

- **If you've experienced a major life change**, such as marriage, buying a home, or starting a business.

- **If you're unsure how to take advantage of certain deductions or tax credits.**

A tax advisor can help you identify opportunities you may not have considered and provide a personalized tax strategy that will allow you to maximize your income and minimize your taxes.

Optimizing your taxes is an essential part of effective financial management. By learning how to take advantage of deductions, tax credits, and investment-related tax benefits, you can significantly reduce the amount of taxes you pay each year. Remember that tax planning is an ongoing process, and staying informed about changes in legislation and tax opportunities will allow you to continuously improve your financial situation. With a well-designed tax strategy, you can maximize your income and use that extra money to achieve your financial goals.

Chapter 12: Plan Your Retirement Starting Today

How to Ensure a Stable Economic Future

Retirement planning is one of the most important aspects of personal financial management. Although many people tend to delay preparing for this stage, the earlier you start, the easier it will be to ensure a stable economic future. Proper planning will allow you to maintain your quality of life during retirement without worrying about financial problems. In this chapter, we will explore how you can start planning for retirement today with practical strategies to build a solid fund that will provide peace of mind in the future.

12.1. Why is Retirement Planning Important?

Retirement is a stage in life where, ideally, you should be able to enjoy your free time and the activities you love without the concern of needing to work for financial support. However, for many people, this phase can become a source of anxiety if they do not have enough financial resources to cover their expenses.

Some of the main reasons to start planning for retirement today include:

- **Longevity**: People are living longer than ever before, meaning you may need enough money to cover 20 to 30 years of expenses after you stop working.

- **Financial Security**: Retirement planning gives you the security of knowing you'll have the financial resources to support yourself in case you're unable to work.

- **Protection from Unexpected Events**: Saving for retirement also protects you from unexpected expenses, such as medical emergencies or long-term care costs.

12.2. Define Your Retirement Goals

The first step in planning for retirement is defining your goals. How do you envision your life after retiring? Your objectives will depend on your desired lifestyle, where you plan to live, whether you want to travel, maintain your home, or even start a new personal project.

Some key questions to help define your retirement goals include:

- At what age would I like to retire?
- How much money will I need to maintain my lifestyle in retirement?
- Do I want to travel or enjoy hobbies that require more income?
- What level of healthcare will I need?

Answering these questions will help you create a clear vision of what your retirement will look like and, consequently, estimate how much money you'll need to save to achieve your goals.

12.3. Calculate How Much You'll Need for Retirement

Once you have a clear idea of your goals, the next step is to calculate how much money you'll need to cover your expenses during retirement. There are several ways to do this, but a commonly used rule is the 80% rule, which suggests you will need about 80% of your current income to maintain your standard of living once you retire.

However, this figure can vary depending on your personal circumstances. If you plan to live more modestly in retirement, you may need less, but if you plan to travel extensively or enjoy a more expensive lifestyle, you might need more than 80%.

A more precise way to calculate how much you'll need is to create an estimated budget for your future expenses, including:

- **Housing expenses**: Rent or mortgage, utility bills, home maintenance.
- **Medical expenses**: Health insurance, medications, long-term care.
- **Transportation**: Whether you'll maintain a car or rely on public transport.
- **Leisure and entertainment**: Travel, hobbies, recreational activities.

Then, you can multiply these annual expenses by the number of years you expect to be retired, which will give you an approximate figure of what you'll need in total.

12.4. Start Saving as Soon as Possible: The Power of Compound Interest

One of the most important principles of retirement planning is to start saving as soon as possible. The earlier you begin, the more time you'll have for your money to grow through the power of compound interest. Compound interest is the process where your savings generate interest, and that interest, in turn, generates more interest. Over time, this creates a cumulative effect that can significantly boost your savings.

For example, if you start saving at age 25 and contribute a small amount each month, you could have a substantial amount by the time you retire, thanks to the effects of compound interest. If you start at age 40 or 50, although you can still save a significant amount, you will need to make larger contributions to reach your goals.

12.5. Use Retirement Savings Accounts

There are several retirement savings accounts that allow you to save efficiently and gain tax benefits while doing so. These plans vary depending on the country, but they are generally designed to help you save long-term while deferring taxes on your contributions or your gains.

Some of the most common retirement accounts include:

12.5.1. Pension Plans (Spain)

In Spain, pension plans are one of the main tools for saving for retirement. Contributions you make to a pension plan are tax-deductible, meaning you can reduce your taxable base and pay fewer taxes in the present. Additionally, the gains generated by these plans are not subject to taxes until you withdraw the money in the future.

Pension plans allow you to invest in a variety of assets, such as stocks, bonds, and investment funds, offering you the opportunity to grow your money over time.

12.5.2. IRAs and 401(k)s (United States)

In the United States, IRAs (Individual Retirement Accounts) and 401(k)s are the most popular accounts for saving for retirement. These accounts offer tax benefits both for contributions and for gains, making them an effective option for long-term savings.

- **Traditional IRA and 401(k)**: Contributions are tax-deductible in the present, and you won't pay taxes on the money until you withdraw it in retirement.
- **Roth IRA and Roth 401(k)**: Contributions are not deductible in the present, but the money grows tax-free, and

you won't pay taxes when you withdraw the funds in retirement.

12.5.3. Retirement Investment Funds

Retirement investment funds are another attractive option for those who want to grow their savings safely over time. Investment funds allow you to diversify your assets, which reduces risk and maximizes long-term returns. There are funds specifically designed for retirement that automatically adjust the composition of assets as you approach the retirement date, reducing risk as you age.

12.6. Investment Strategies for Retirement

As you save for retirement, it's important to adopt an investment strategy that allows you to grow your money efficiently and safely. Here are some basic investment strategies for retirement:

12.6.1. Diversification

Diversification is key to minimizing risk in your investments. By diversifying, you spread your money across different types of assets, such as stocks, bonds, real estate, and cash. This protects you from market volatility since if one type of asset performs poorly, the others can offset those losses.

12.6.2. Index Funds

Index funds are a popular option for retirement savers because they allow you to invest in a broad set of assets automatically and at a low cost. These funds track a market index, such as the S&P 500, allowing you to benefit from overall market growth without needing to choose individual stocks.

12.6.3. Bond Investments

As you approach retirement, it's advisable to start reducing the risk in your investment portfolio. Bonds are a safer investment than stocks as they offer stable income and are less volatile. Investing in bonds will help you preserve your capital while still earning interest income.

12.7. Adjust Your Contributions Based on Your Age

The amount you need to save for retirement will largely depend on your age and when you plan to retire. If you start saving at an early age, you can make smaller contributions and benefit from long-term growth. However, if you start later, you'll need to make larger contributions to reach your goals.

Here are some general recommendations:

- **20 to 30 years old**: At this stage, you have the advantage of time, so you can save small amounts consistently and take advantage of compound interest. Investing in higher-risk assets, such as stocks, is a good strategy since you have time to recover from any market downturns.

- **30 to 50 years old**: As you approach mid-career, it's advisable to increase your contributions to your retirement accounts and start adjusting your portfolio to reduce risk. You can still invest in growth assets, but it's also important to include bonds and other safer assets.

- **50 years old and up**: At this stage, you should focus on maximizing your savings and protecting what you've already accumulated. Increase your contributions if possible, and adjust your investments to reduce risk as you approach retirement.

12.8. Prepare a Plan for Medical Expenses

One of the largest expenses retirees face is healthcare costs. It's crucial to plan for how you'll cover these costs, which include health insurance, medications, and potential long-term care expenses.

Some ways to prepare for these costs include:

- **Make sure you have adequate health insurance**: Research what insurance options will be available to you when you retire and plan accordingly. In many countries, such as the United States, you can opt for programs like Medicare, but you'll still need to cover additional expenses.
- **Contribute to health savings accounts**: In some countries, there are specialized savings accounts for medical expenses, such as HSAs (Health Savings Accounts) in the United States. These accounts allow you to save for future medical expenses with tax advantages.

12.9. The Importance of Flexibility in Your Retirement Plan

A good retirement plan must be flexible and adjustable as your circumstances change. Over the years, your goals or needs may change, so it's important to review and adjust your plan regularly. For example, you may decide to work a few more years than initially planned or change your investment strategy as you approach retirement.

Having a flexible plan will allow you to adapt to market fluctuations, changes in your personal situation, and other factors that could affect your retirement savings.

12.10. Maintain Financial Education During Retirement

Finally, once you reach retirement, it's essential to continue learning about financial management to ensure your savings last. This includes managing your investments, monitoring your expenses, and making adjustments as necessary. Maintaining good financial education will allow you to enjoy a worry-free retirement.

Planning your retirement today is one of the most important decisions you can make to ensure a stable economic future. By defining your goals, calculating how much you'll need, starting to save early, and taking advantage of tax-advantaged retirement accounts, you'll be on the right path to achieving financial security in this stage of life. Remember that consistency and flexibility are key: the earlier you start and the better you adjust your plan over time, the easier it will be to achieve your retirement goals.

Chapter 13: How to Avoid Common Financial Mistakes

What You Should Know to Avoid Economic Pitfalls

Personal finance is a fundamental aspect of our lives, and while we all strive for economic stability, it's easy to fall into financial mistakes that can compromise our long-term well-being. Common financial errors may seem minor at the moment, but over time, they can have a significant impact on your finances, causing stress and making it difficult to achieve your goals. The key to avoiding these mistakes is to have a solid financial education and be aware of the risks and pitfalls that exist in money management.

In this chapter, we will explore some of the most common financial mistakes people tend to make and how to avoid them to ensure a stable and prosperous economic future.

13.1. Living Beyond Your Means

One of the most common and dangerous mistakes is living beyond your means. This means spending more money than you actually earn, often resorting to credit or cards to finance a lifestyle you cannot afford. This behavior quickly leads to debt and can become a difficult cycle to break.

How to avoid it:

- **Budget your expenses**: Create a realistic budget that matches your income. Ensure that your essential expenses, such as housing, food, and transportation, do not exceed 50% of your income.

- **Prioritize saving**: Develop the habit of saving before spending on non-essential items. At least 20% of your income should go toward savings or investments.

- **Avoid impulse purchases**: Before making a significant purchase, give yourself time to assess whether you truly need the item or service. The 24-hour rule can help you avoid unnecessary spending.

13.2. Accumulating Credit Card Debt

Overusing credit cards is one of the most common and damaging financial mistakes. Credit cards can be useful when used responsibly, but misuse can lead to debt that's difficult to repay due to high-interest rates. Paying only the minimum balance each month leads to interest accumulation, increasing the overall cost of what you purchased.

How to avoid it:

- **Pay the full balance each month**: If you use a credit card, ensure you pay the full balance each month to avoid interest. Don't use the card as an extension of your income.

- **Limit its use**: Reserve your credit card for emergencies or purchases you can pay off immediately. If you tend to overspend, consider using a debit card instead.

- **Be cautious with credit offers**: Don't automatically accept every credit offer you receive. More cards mean more temptation to spend.

13.3. Not Having an Emergency Fund

One of the most common mistakes is not having an emergency fund. Many people are comfortable living paycheck to paycheck, but when an unexpected expense arises (like car repairs or medical emergencies), they are forced to go into debt to cover it. An emergency fund allows you to handle these unexpected events without resorting to loans or credit cards.

How to avoid it:

- **Build a solid emergency fund**: A good emergency fund should cover three to six months of your essential expenses. Start with small contributions and gradually build your fund to meet that goal.
- **Make saving a priority**: Automate your savings so that a portion of your income is automatically transferred to your emergency fund.

13.4. Not Planning for Retirement

One of the costliest long-term mistakes is not planning for retirement. Many people, especially younger individuals, tend to think they have plenty of time to start saving for retirement, but the longer you wait, the harder it will be to accumulate the necessary funds to support yourself once you stop working.

How to avoid it:

- **Start saving as early as possible**: Take advantage of compound interest by starting to save for retirement as soon as possible. Even small contributions can grow significantly over time.
- **Contribute to retirement plans**: If your employer offers a retirement plan, such as a 401(k) or pension plan, make sure to contribute as much as possible. You can also open an IRA or similar account for independent savings.

13.5. Not Having a Financial Plan

Living without a financial plan is like navigating without a compass. Many people simply go from month to month without clear goals, spending their money on what seems necessary at the time but without thinking about long-term objectives. This leads to disorganized financial management and can hinder the achievement of important goals such as buying a house, saving for retirement, or eliminating debt.

How to avoid it:

- **Set clear financial goals**: Define short, medium, and long-term financial goals, such as paying off debt, saving for a house, or building a retirement fund. These goals will provide you with a clear guide to managing your money.

- **Create an action plan**: Once you have your goals, create a plan to achieve them. This may involve cutting expenses, increasing your income, or changing your savings and investment strategy.

13.6. Not Diversifying Investments

When you start investing, one of the most common mistakes is not diversifying. Putting all your eggs in one basket—investing all your money in a single stock, sector, or type of asset—increases the risk that a downturn in that sector or company could severely impact your portfolio.

How to avoid it:

- **Diversify your investments**: Spread your money across different types of assets (stocks, bonds, real estate, etc.) and sectors. This reduces risk and increases the chances of consistent returns.

- **Consider mutual funds or ETFs**: If you lack experience selecting individual stocks, index funds or ETFs are excellent options to automatically diversify your portfolio.

13.7. Ignoring Small Expenses

Daily small expenses, such as coffees, subscriptions, or impulse purchases, may seem insignificant, but over time they add up to a considerable amount that can harm your finances. Ignoring these small expenses is a common financial mistake that may leave you wondering where your money went at the end of the month.

How to avoid it:

- **Track all your expenses**: Keep track of every expense, no matter how small. This will allow you to see clearly where you are spending and identify areas where you could save.
- **Cut or eliminate unnecessary expenses**: Review your spending and cut out things that do not add value to your life. Small adjustments, like making coffee at home or canceling an unused subscription, can make a big difference over time.

13.8. Not Having Adequate Insurance

Insurance is a key financial tool to protect your assets, but many people underestimate its importance or don't have enough coverage. Not having insurance or being underinsured can be devastating if you face a medical emergency, a car accident, or a natural disaster.

How to avoid it:

- **Ensure you have adequate coverage**: Review your financial situation and ensure you have enough health, life, home, and car insurance to protect your assets.

- **Review your policies regularly**: As your life changes (buying a home, having a child, increasing income), your insurance policies should adjust as well.

13.9. Making Financial Decisions Without Information

Making major financial decisions, such as buying a house, investing, or taking out a loan, without doing adequate research can lead to costly mistakes. Impulsive or emotion-based decisions can put your financial stability at risk.

How to avoid it:

- **Get informed before making major decisions**: Research all the options available before making a significant financial decision. Consult financial advisors, read about the topic, and ensure you understand all the risks involved.

- **Be patient**: Don't make impulsive financial decisions. Take the time to analyze all the variables and consider the long-term impact.

13.10. Not Adjusting Your Lifestyle to Income Changes

A common mistake is increasing your lifestyle as your income rises, also known as lifestyle inflation. While it's natural to want to enjoy an increase in income, doing so without moderation can prevent you from saving more or investing in your future.

How to avoid it:

- **Keep your expenses in check**: As your income increases, avoid automatically increasing your expenses. Instead, use a significant portion of the increase to save or invest.

- **Prioritize your financial goals**: If you receive a bonus or salary raise, use it to move closer to your long-term financial goals, such as paying off debt or increasing your retirement fund.

Avoiding common financial mistakes is key to building a solid and successful economic life. With proper financial education, planning, and self-discipline, you can prevent these errors and manage your money wisely, achieving your goals without falling into economic traps. The first step in avoiding these mistakes is to be aware of them and make informed decisions that will help you improve your financial situation in the long term.

Chapter 14: Relationships and Money: A Crucial Balance

How Money Affects Your Relationships and How to Manage It

Money is a sensitive subject that has the power to profoundly affect our personal relationships. Whether with your partner, family, friends, or business associates, the way we manage money can influence trust, communication, and emotional stability. Financial issues are often a primary cause of tension in relationships, but with good management and open communication, it's possible to find a balance that strengthens both your financial well-being and your relationships.

In this chapter, we'll explore how money impacts relationship dynamics and offer strategies for managing finances intelligently and harmoniously so that they don't become a source of conflict.

14.1. The Impact of Money on Relationships

Although money is just a tool, it can symbolize many things within a relationship: security, power, control, and sometimes even love or success. Differences in financial habits, expectations, and beliefs about money can create tensions that, if not properly managed, can deteriorate the relationship.

Some of the most common ways money impacts relationships include:

- **Financial Inequality**: Differences in income can create power imbalances in the relationship, where one person may feel controlled or undervalued due to their financial situation.

- **Shared Financial Stress**: When both partners face financial problems, such as debt or unexpected expenses, shared stress can increase pressure and lead to arguments.
- **Different Money Philosophies**: Some people are savers while others prefer to spend. When these approaches clash in a relationship, finding middle ground without compromising harmony can be challenging.

14.2. The Importance of Financial Communication

Open and honest communication about money is essential to maintaining a healthy and balanced relationship. However, many people avoid talking about finances, either due to discomfort or fear of conflict. This silence can lead to misunderstandings, resentment, and a lack of trust.

How to Encourage Financial Communication:

- **Talk about Money Early On**: It's important for couples to discuss money early in their relationship to understand each other's financial beliefs, habits, and goals. This helps avoid unpleasant surprises later on.
- **Set Regular Financial Meetings**: Schedule periodic meetings to discuss finances, review budgets, set goals, and resolve financial issues, ensuring that both partners feel involved and aligned in financial management.
- **Be Honest About Debts and Expenses**: Both partners should be completely transparent about their debts, spending habits, and financial concerns. Hiding debts or expenses can lead to distrust and worsen problems.

14.3. Managing Finances as a Couple: Options and Strategies

One of the most important decisions couples need to make is how to manage their finances together. There are various approaches, and the key is to find the one that best suits the relationship's dynamic.

Options for Managing Finances as a Couple:

- **Joint Accounts**: In this approach, all income and expenses are managed through a shared bank account. This is ideal for couples who want fully integrated and transparent financial management, although it requires a high level of trust and constant communication.

- **Separate Accounts**: Some couples prefer to keep their bank accounts separate, allowing for a degree of financial independence. This approach can be helpful when partners have different spending habits or unequal incomes.

- **Mixed Accounts**: A mixed approach involves having a joint account for shared expenses, like rent, bills, or shared savings, while each partner maintains a separate account for personal expenses.

How to Choose the Right Approach:

- **Evaluate Each Other's Financial Habits**: If both partners have similar financial philosophies, a joint account may work well. Conversely, if they have significant differences in financial approaches, separate or mixed accounts can offer more flexibility.

- **Consider Income Inequality**: If one partner earns significantly more than the other, it's important to find a fair system to avoid resentment. For example, some couples opt to contribute to shared expenses in proportion to their incomes instead of splitting them equally.

- **Set Shared Goals**: Regardless of the approach chosen, establishing shared financial goals is essential. Whether it's saving for a home, planning for retirement, or paying off debt, having clear goals will help both partners work in the same direction.

14.4. The Role of Money in Family Relationships

Money can also create tensions in family relationships. Whether between parents and children, siblings, or extended relatives, financial dynamics can be complex and charged with emotions.

Common Issues in Family Relationships:

- **Family Loans**: Lending or borrowing money from family members can risk the relationship if expectations and terms aren't managed properly. If a family member can't repay the loan or if there's a misunderstanding, resentment may grow.
- **Unequal Financial Support**: In some families, one member may feel they receive less financial support than others, which can create conflicts and dissatisfaction.
- **Inheritances**: The distribution of inheritances is another sensitive issue that can cause tensions among family members. Disputes over fairness in the distribution of assets or a lack of planning can cause deep divisions within the family.

How to Avoid Financial Problems in the Family:

- **Set Clear Rules for Loans**: If you decide to lend money to a family member, be sure to clearly define the terms of the agreement, including the amount, repayment period, and expectations. Ideally, put it in writing to avoid misunderstandings.
- **Be Honest About Your Expectations**: If you can't afford to lend money or provide financial support, be honest from

the start. It's essential to set healthy boundaries to avoid compromising your financial stability.

- **Plan for Inheritance**: If you are in a position to plan the distribution of your assets, consider doing so in a clear and fair manner, involving family members in the process to avoid surprises or misunderstandings.

14.5. Friendship and Money: Finding Balance

Money can also test friendships. Loans between friends, shared expenses, or differences in lifestyle can create tensions and lead to relationship deterioration.

Common Issues in Friendships:

- **Loans Between Friends**: Lending money to friends can endanger the relationship if funds aren't repaid or if there are misunderstandings about the agreement.

- **Differences in Lifestyle**: When friends have different income levels, it can be challenging to maintain a balanced relationship. Those with higher incomes may feel frustrated about covering more expenses, while those with lower incomes may feel embarrassed or uncomfortable.

- **Shared Expenses**: Outings or shared vacations with friends can create conflicts if there isn't a clear agreement on how costs will be divided.

How to Manage Money in Friendships:

- **Avoid Lending Large Sums of Money**: If you decide to lend money to a friend, make sure it's an amount you can afford to lose without affecting the relationship. Another option is to offer the money as a gift instead of a loan if the situation allows.

- **Be Honest About Your Financial Limits**: If you can't afford your friends' lifestyle, be clear and honest about your financial boundaries. There's nothing wrong with setting limits when it comes to expenses.

- **Set Clear Rules for Shared Expenses**: When planning outings or trips with friends, ensure everyone agrees on how costs will be divided. This will prevent misunderstandings and resentments later on.

14.6. Financial Stress: How It Affects Your Relationships

Financial stress not only affects your economic well-being but can also have a direct impact on the health of your relationships. When money is a constant source of stress, it's easy for arguments to arise, and people can feel overwhelmed.

How to Handle Financial Stress in Relationships:

- **Talk Openly About Your Concerns**: If you're feeling stressed about your financial situation, talk to your partner or the person involved. Sharing your concerns can often relieve some of the stress and lead to joint solutions.

- **Set a Joint Financial Plan**: Creating a solid and realistic financial plan can significantly reduce stress. Knowing that both partners are working toward the same financial goals can bring peace of mind.

- **Seek Help if Needed**: If you feel that financial stress is seriously affecting your relationship, consider seeking outside help. A financial advisor or therapist can offer you strategies to improve your situation and reduce tension.

14.7. Strengthening Relationships Through Financial Management

While money can be a source of conflict, it can also be a powerful tool for strengthening relationships when managed correctly. Shared financial management can foster a greater sense of teamwork and commitment, generating trust and unity.

Strategies to Strengthen Relationships Through Money:

- **Work on Joint Financial Goals**: Setting and achieving shared financial goals, such as saving for a home or planning a trip, can strengthen your relationship and create a sense of mutual accomplishment.

- **Celebrate Financial Achievements Together**: Whether paying off debt, reaching a savings goal, or investing in something important, it's essential to celebrate financial achievements together. These celebrations reinforce connection and cooperation.

- **Develop Healthy Financial Habits**: Fostering healthy financial habits, such as disciplined saving or investing, will not only improve your economic stability but also promote communication and teamwork.

The balance between money and relationships is essential to maintaining harmony and stability in all areas of life. With open communication, clear expectations, and proper financial management, it's possible to avoid conflicts and use money as a tool to strengthen bonds. By proactively addressing money with mutual respect, you can ensure that personal relationships and economic well-being thrive together.

Chapter 15: Building Your Financial Future: The Long-Term Plan

Creating a Comprehensive Plan for Financial Security

Achieving a stable financial future is not the result of luck, but of deliberate and well-executed planning. Developing a long-term financial plan enables you to take control of your finances, ensure that your goals are met, and prepare for any unforeseen circumstances that may arise along the way. Crafting a comprehensive plan not only ensures that you can enjoy a comfortable life during retirement but also gives you peace of mind knowing your finances are in order.

In this chapter, we'll guide you step-by-step through the key strategies for building a comprehensive financial plan to secure your future—from defining your goals to executing and adjusting your financial decisions over time.

15.1. Define Your Long-Term Financial Goals

The first step to building your financial future is setting clear and realistic goals. A good long-term financial plan should be based on specific objectives that guide you through life and keep you focused on what you want to achieve. Financial goals can vary significantly from person to person, but some of the most common include:

- **Saving for Retirement**: This is a primary goal for most people. Your plan should include long-term saving and investment strategies to ensure you have enough money to maintain your lifestyle when you stop working.

- **Buying a Home or Paying Off a Mortgage**: Homeownership is a long-term financial goal for many, whether it's buying a home for the first time or paying off a mortgage completely.

- **Funding Children's Education**: For parents, ensuring their children have access to quality education can be a key financial goal.

- **Building a Solid Emergency Fund**: An emergency fund protects you from unexpected events and gives you peace of mind by preparing you for any eventuality.

How to Define Your Goals:

- **Be Specific**: Instead of saying, "I want to save for retirement," define how much money you'll need for your ideal retirement and when you plan to start retiring.

- **Set a Timeframe for Your Goals**: Each goal should have a timeline, whether it's short-, medium-, or long-term. For example, saving for a car in three years or planning for retirement in 25 years.

- **Prioritize Your Goals**: You'll likely have multiple financial goals at once, so it's important to prioritize them. Rank your goals by importance and timeframe, focusing on the most critical ones first, like creating an emergency fund or paying off high-interest debt.

15.2. Create a Budget to Manage Your Income and Expenses

One of the most essential tools for building a stable financial future is creating a budget. A budget allows you to control your income and expenses, live within your means, and work towards achieving your long-term goals.

How to Create an Effective Budget:

- **Assess Your Net Income**: The first step is knowing your net income—the money you have available after taxes and deductions.

- **Classify Your Expenses**: Divide your expenses into two categories: essentials (like housing, food, transportation, etc.) and discretionary spending (like entertainment, clothing, outings). This will help you see clearly where you can adjust expenses if necessary.

- **Apply the 50/30/20 Rule**: As discussed in previous chapters, the 50/30/20 rule is a good guide for allocating your income: 50% for needs, 30% for wants, and 20% for savings or debt payments.

- **Adjust Your Budget According to Your Goals**: Ensure your budget includes regular contributions toward your savings goals, like retirement, education, or your emergency fund.

15.3. Save and Invest for the Future

Saving and investing are two cornerstones of a long-term financial plan. Saving money is essential for building a solid financial foundation, while investing allows you to grow that money over time. Both elements should work together to secure your economic future.

Saving Strategies:

- **Automate Your Savings**: Set up automatic transfers to a savings account each month to ensure you consistently contribute to your emergency fund and other financial goals.

- **Emergency Fund**: Before you start investing, make sure you have an emergency fund that covers at least three to six months of basic expenses.

Investment Strategies:

- **Diversify Your Investments**: Diversifying your portfolio is key to reducing risk. Ensure you spread your investments across different asset types, like stocks, bonds, real estate, and cash.

- **Invest for the Long Term**: The key to long-term investment success is patience. Maintain a stable investment strategy and avoid reacting emotionally to market fluctuations.

- **Take Advantage of Tax Benefits**: Contribute to tax-advantaged investment accounts, like retirement savings plans (IRAs or 401(k)s in the U.S.) or specific plans in your country.

15.4. Debt Management: Freeing Yourself from Financial Burdens

A crucial step to building a solid financial future is managing and eliminating debt. Debt, especially high-interest debt, can be a significant barrier to achieving your long-term financial goals. The sooner you free yourself from debt, the more money you'll have available for saving and investing.

How to Manage Debt:

- **Prioritize High-Interest Debts**: Pay off debts with the highest interest rates first, like credit card debt. These debts are the most detrimental to your savings capacity.

- **Consolidate Your Debts If Possible**: If you have multiple high-interest debts, consider consolidating them into a single loan with a lower interest rate. This will simplify your payments and may reduce the total interest you pay.

- **Avoid Taking On New Debt**: Once you're working on paying off your current debts, it's essential to avoid accumulating new ones unless absolutely necessary (for example, a mortgage or student loan).

15.5. Protect Your Future with Adequate Insurance

Another essential aspect of a comprehensive financial plan is having the right insurance coverage. Insurance protects you from unexpected events and ensures that you won't need to dip into your savings or investments in case of an emergency.

Important Types of Insurance to Consider:

- **Health Insurance**: Medical emergencies can be extremely costly, so having good health insurance is essential to protect your financial well-being.

- **Life Insurance**: If you have dependents, life insurance can ensure that your loved ones are financially protected if something happens to you.

- **Disability Insurance**: This insurance protects you if you lose the ability to work due to illness or accident, ensuring you have income to cover basic expenses.

- **Homeowner's or Renter's Insurance**: Protects your home or belongings against unexpected damage or theft, ensuring you won't have to spend large sums on repairs or replacements.

15.6. Start Planning for Retirement Today

We've previously discussed the importance of retirement planning in detail, but it's essential to reiterate it as a vital part of your long-term financial plan. The sooner you start saving for retirement, the better prepared you'll be for the future.

Key Steps for Retirement Planning:

- **Regularly Contribute to a Retirement Plan**: If your employer offers a retirement plan with matching contributions, take full advantage. You can also open additional accounts, such as an Individual Retirement Account (IRA) or private pension plan.

- **Adjust Your Investments as You Age**: As you approach retirement, it's advisable to reduce the risk in your investment portfolio by opting for safer assets, like bonds.

15.7. Review and Adjust Your Plan Periodically

A long-term financial plan is not static. Throughout your life, your circumstances, goals, and priorities will change, so it's important to review and adjust your plan periodically to ensure it remains aligned with your objectives.

How to Review and Adjust Your Plan:

- **Review Your Plan Annually**: At least once a year, review your budget, investments, insurance, and goals to ensure everything is in order. Adjust your savings or investment contributions as needed.

- **Adapt to Major Life Changes**: Major life changes like marriage, the birth of a child, a job change, or buying a home may require adjustments to your financial plan.

- **Consult a Financial Advisor**: If you face complex decisions or are unsure how to adjust your plan, consult a financial advisor. An expert can offer you a clear and objective perspective.

15.8. Maintain a Long-Term Mind-set

Building a solid financial future requires patience, discipline, and a long-term mind-set. Avoid impulsive decisions and stay focused on your goals. Temporary financial setbacks may arise, but if you stick to your plan and make necessary adjustments, you'll be prepared to face any challenge.

Tips for Maintaining a Long-Term Mind-set:

- **Avoid Emotional Decisions**: Don't make financial decisions based on emotions, like panic selling investments during a market downturn. Stay calm and trust your plan.

- **Celebrate Small Achievements**: As you reach intermediate financial goals, like paying off debt or hitting a savings milestone, celebrate those achievements. This will motivate you to keep moving toward your bigger goals.

Building a stable financial future is a process that requires time, effort, and careful planning. By setting clear goals, creating a solid budget, saving and investing wisely, managing debt, and protecting yourself with insurance, you'll be on the right path toward financial security. Remember that financial success isn't achieved overnight, but with a disciplined and consistent approach, you can create a future filled with possibilities and peace of mind.

Chapter 16: The Importance of Financial Legacy and Estate Planning

How to Ensure Your Wealth Transcends Future Generations

Estate planning is a key component of a comprehensive financial plan, as it ensures that your assets and resources are managed according to your wishes and transferred efficiently to future generations. It's not just about wealth distribution; it's about ensuring your loved ones are protected and your legacy endures. Proper estate planning reduces family conflicts, minimizes tax burdens, and ensures the continuity of your projects and values.

In this chapter, we'll cover what estate planning entails, why it's essential to create a plan, and how you can manage and protect your financial legacy to ensure the security and stability of your loved ones.

16.1. What Is Estate Planning?

Estate planning is the process of organizing the management and distribution of your estate—including financial assets, properties, investments, and other belongings—during your life and after your death. This planning involves decisions about who will inherit your assets, how they'll be distributed, and when. The main goal is to protect your family, ensure proper management of your estate, and avoid potential legal or tax issues in the future.

A well-structured estate plan should include several key components, such as a will, trusts, powers of attorney, and advance healthcare directives.

16.2. Why Is Estate Planning Important?

Estate planning is crucial not only for individuals with substantial wealth but for anyone wishing to protect their loved ones and ensure their assets are managed properly. Without an estate plan, your assets could be subject to family disputes, high tax burdens, or be handled against your wishes.

Some key reasons to plan your estate include:

- **Protecting Your Loved Ones**: An estate plan ensures that your family members or designated individuals inherit your assets according to your wishes, avoiding possible disputes or misunderstandings.

- **Minimizing Taxes**: A well-structured estate plan can reduce estate, gift, and inheritance taxes, thus preserving the value of your assets for your heirs.

- **Continuity of Your Projects**: If you have a business or projects you wish to continue after your death, estate planning ensures these initiatives remain uninterrupted.

- **Control Over Medical Decisions**: Through advance healthcare directives, you can establish instructions on the type of medical care you want if you become unable to make decisions for yourself.

16.3. Essential Components of an Estate Plan

An effective estate plan should include a series of documents and strategies to ensure your assets are managed efficiently. Below are the essential components you should consider:

16.3.1. Will

The will is the cornerstone of any estate plan. It details how you want your assets distributed after your death. A well-written will prevents the law from deciding who receives your assets and reduces the likelihood of family conflicts.

It's important that your will is clear and specific, stating not only who will receive each asset but also how and when. It should be updated periodically, especially after significant events like births, deaths, or changes in your financial situation.

16.3.2. Trusts

A trust is a legal tool that allows you to transfer your assets to a trustee who manages and distributes them according to your instructions. Trusts can offer more flexibility and control than a will, allowing you to specify how and when assets will be distributed.

There are several types of trusts, such as revocable trusts, which can be modified during your lifetime, and irrevocable trusts, which offer greater tax protection but cannot be changed once established. Trusts are also useful for avoiding probate, which can save your heirs time and money.

16.3.3. Powers of Attorney

A power of attorney is a document that allows you to appoint a trusted person to manage your financial and legal affairs if you are unable to do so. There are two main types of powers of attorney:

- **General Power**: Grants the designated person authority to make financial and legal decisions on your behalf.
- **Medical Power**: Allows another person to make medical decisions for you if you become incapacitated.

Having these powers in place ensures that someone you trust can handle your affairs promptly and efficiently in an emergency.

16.3.4. Advance Healthcare Directives

Advance healthcare directives allow you to specify the type of medical care you wish to receive if you cannot communicate your decisions. This can include instructions on medical treatments, cardiopulmonary resuscitation (CPR), or the use of ventilators.

Clearly defining these directives not only protects your wishes but also relieves your loved ones from having to make difficult decisions during a crisis.

16.3.5. Beneficiary Designations on Accounts and Insurance

Be sure to periodically update the beneficiaries on your retirement accounts, life insurance policies, and other investments that include this option. People often forget to review these designations, which could result in funds being distributed against your wishes if circumstances change, such as a divorce or the birth of a child.

16.4. Strategies to Minimize Estate Taxes

One of the most important aspects of estate planning is minimizing estate and inheritance taxes, which can significantly reduce the value of the assets your heirs receive. There are several legal strategies that can help reduce the tax burden on your estate.

16.4.1. Irrevocable Trusts

Irrevocable trusts are an excellent tool for reducing estate taxes, as assets transferred into this type of trust are no longer considered part of your personal estate. This means they are not subject to estate taxes after your death.

16.4.2. Lifetime Gifts

Another strategy to minimize taxes is to make lifetime gifts to your heirs. In many countries, you can give a certain amount of money or assets to your children or relatives each year without being subject to gift taxes. These gifts can reduce the size of your estate and thus lower the taxes that will apply when you pass away.

16.4.3. Life Insurance

Life insurance can also play a crucial role in estate planning. Life insurance payouts are generally tax-exempt, meaning your beneficiaries receive the insured amount without tax deductions. This can be an excellent way to ensure your loved ones have additional financial resources, regardless of the estate taxes that may apply to other assets.

16.5. The Importance of Family Communication in Estate Planning

One of the most common mistakes in estate planning is failing to communicate decisions clearly to heirs and family members. Lack of communication can lead to misunderstandings, conflicts, and resentment among heirs, complicating the succession process.

How to Facilitate Communication:

- **Talk Openly with Your Family**: Share your wishes and the reasons behind your estate planning decisions with your closest family members. This reduces the possibility of disputes and ensures that everyone understands your intentions.

- **Explain the Purpose of Trusts or Specific Decisions**: If you have set up trusts or designated specific beneficiaries, make sure your heirs understand why you made those decisions.

- **Involve a Lawyer or Financial Advisor**: Having a professional help you communicate and document your decisions can make the process clearer and minimize the chance of mistakes or misunderstandings.

16.6. Reviewing and Updating Your Estate Plan

Life changes, and your estate plan should adapt to those changes. It's important to review and update your plan periodically to ensure it still reflects your current wishes and circumstances.

When to Review Your Estate Plan:

- **Family Changes**: If you marry, divorce, have a child, or lose a loved one, it's essential to review your plan to reflect these new circumstances.

- **Changes in Tax Laws**: Tax laws may change, and these modifications can impact the structure of your estate plan. Stay informed about legislative changes and adjust your plan accordingly.

- **Changes in Your Financial Situation**: If you experience a significant increase or decrease in your estate, your plan should reflect these changes to ensure proper distribution of your assets.

16.7. A Financial Legacy Beyond Money

Your financial legacy isn't limited to material wealth; it also includes the values, principles, and lessons you pass down to future generations. It's essential that your estate plan also considers how you want to pass on those values and ensure that your legacy has a positive impact on your loved ones and the community.

How to Leave a Meaningful Legacy:

- **Create Funds for Charitable Causes**: If you are passionate about a cause, consider creating a trust or fund that supports it after your death. This type of legacy can have a lasting impact on the community and perpetuate your values.

- **Involve Your Family in Philanthropic Decisions**: Invite your heirs to participate in decisions related to donations or philanthropic investments. This not only ensures your values endure but also strengthens family unity and purpose.

- **Pass on Financial Education**: Teaching your children and heirs to manage their finances is one of the best ways to ensure your legacy has a positive impact. Good financial education will allow future generations to manage their inheritance responsibly.

Estate planning is an essential process for protecting your loved ones, minimizing conflicts, and ensuring that your wishes are fulfilled after your death. With a well-structured plan that includes a will, trusts, insurance, and tax strategies, you can ensure the continuity of your financial legacy while passing down important values and principles. The key is to review and adjust your plan over time to reflect your changing circumstances and desires

Chapter 17: The Importance of Financial Flexibility in Times of Uncertainty

How to Adapt and Protect Your Finances in Difficult Times

Life is unpredictable, and periods of uncertainty can arise without warning, whether in the form of economic crises, job loss, pandemics, or significant personal changes. In such times, financial flexibility becomes a crucial tool to protect your finances, stay afloat, and adapt to new circumstances. The ability to adjust your short- and long-term financial plan provides not only peace of mind but also prepares you to face whatever challenges life presents.

In this chapter, we will explore what financial flexibility is, why it's essential in uncertain times, and how you can structure your finances to be more resilient and adaptable to unexpected changes.

17.1 What Is Financial Flexibility?

Financial flexibility is the ability to adjust and adapt your personal finances according to changing circumstances. This adaptability enables you to respond effectively to crises, both large and small, minimizing the negative impact on your finances and helping you maintain control over your resources.

Some examples of financial flexibility include:

- Temporarily reducing expenses when income decreases.
- Adjusting saving or investment priorities based on economic conditions.

- Quickly accessing funds in case of an emergency.

Having financial flexibility doesn't mean living under constant restrictions; it means having a system that allows for quick adjustments without compromising long-term stability.

17.2 The Importance of Financial Flexibility in Times of Uncertainty

Uncertain times can present themselves in various forms, such as economic recessions, changes in the job market, or unforeseen events in your personal life. If you don't have a flexible plan, these situations can quickly destabilize your finances. On the other hand, with a structured and adaptable financial system, you can mitigate the impact of uncertainty and maintain a more secure financial position.

Key reasons financial flexibility is crucial during uncertain times include:

- **Protecting Your Lifestyle**: Financial flexibility allows you to adjust expenses without severely impacting your quality of life or financial goals.

- **Avoiding Unnecessary Debt**: When circumstances change, flexibility helps you avoid relying on emergency loans or accumulating debt for unforeseen expenses.

- **Maintaining Emotional Stability**: Financial uncertainty can cause stress and anxiety. Having a flexible plan gives you the peace of mind of knowing you're prepared to face adversity without losing control of your finances.

17.3 Strategies to Build Financial Flexibility

Achieving financial flexibility requires a comprehensive approach that includes intelligent management of your income, expenses, savings, and investments. Below are key strategies to structure your finances to be flexible and adaptable:

17.3.1 Build a Solid Emergency Fund

A well-established emergency fund is one of the pillars of financial flexibility. This fund provides a safety net you can rely on during crises, such as job loss, unexpected repairs, or medical emergencies.

How to Build an Emergency Fund:

- **Save Three to Six Months of Essential Expenses**: This is the minimum goal for your emergency fund. If you have an unstable income or rely on a single salary, it's advisable to save even more.

- **Keep It Liquid**: The emergency fund should be in a savings account or a financial instrument that is easily accessible. It should not be invested in volatile assets, like stocks, that could lose value during a crisis.

17.3.2 Review and Adjust Your Budget Regularly

The ability to adjust your budget according to circumstances is essential to maintaining financial flexibility. If you go through uncertain times, such as an income reduction, your budget should be adaptable enough to reflect this new reality without endangering your long-term stability.

How to Maintain a Flexible Budget:

- **Identify Your Essential Expenses**: Classify your expenses into essential (housing, food, transportation) and discretionary (entertainment, travel). In uncertain times, it's easier to reduce or eliminate discretionary expenses.

- **Conduct Regular Reviews**: Review your budget quarterly or whenever you experience a significant change in income or expenses. Adjust expense categories according to the new situation.

- **Create an Alternative Spending Plan**: In addition to your usual budget, it's helpful to have an "emergency" spending plan for times of crisis. This plan should outline which expenses you'd cut first and what additional measures you could take.

17.3.3 Diversify Your Income Sources

Relying on a single income source can be risky, especially during uncertain times. If you lose your job or your sector faces difficulties, you could be left without stable income. Diversifying your income gives you greater protection and the flexibility to make adjustments if one of those sources decreases or disappears.

How to Diversify Your Income:

- **Develop Freelance or Side Skills**: Consider developing skills you can use in the freelance market or to earn secondary income, such as consulting, online teaching, or creative work.

- **Explore Passive Income Sources**: Passive income sources, such as rental income, stock dividends, or digital content creation, can provide steady income without requiring full-time commitment.

17.3.4 Keep Debt to a Minimum and Manage It Wisely

One of the biggest barriers to financial flexibility is excessive debt. When you're committed to paying off high-interest debt, you have less ability to adjust your expenses or save during uncertain times.

How to Manage Debt:

- **Prioritize High-Interest Debt**: Credit cards or personal loans usually have higher interest rates. Pay them off as soon as possible to free up resources and improve your flexibility.

- **Avoid New Debt in Uncertain Times**: During uncertain times, it's best to avoid taking on unnecessary debt. If possible, use your emergency fund instead of taking out loans.

17.3.5 Invest Flexibly

Investments can be a source of income and long-term growth, but in uncertain times, it's essential to have a flexible investment strategy that can adapt to market fluctuations.

How to Invest Flexibly:

- **Diversify Your Portfolio**: Diversification protects you from market fluctuations. Keep a balanced mix of assets, such as stocks, bonds, and real estate, to reduce risk.
- **Maintain Liquidity in Your Portfolio**: In addition to long-term investments, it's important to keep part of your portfolio in liquid assets that you can quickly sell if you need cash, such as bond funds or money market funds.

17.4 The Importance of Mind-set in Uncertain Times

Financial flexibility depends not only on numbers but also on your mind-set. Being able to make rational decisions and adapt to changes without panic is essential for maintaining financial stability during difficult times.

Keys to Developing a Flexible Financial Mind-set:

- **Embrace Uncertainty**: Uncertainty is an inevitable part of life. Instead of fearing it, accept that changes will occur and plan accordingly.
- **Be Proactive Rather than Reactive**: In times of uncertainty, anticipate potential financial problems instead of waiting for them to happen. If you see that your industry

is at risk, start saving more, reduce expenses, or seek new income sources before the crisis directly affects you.

- **Stay Calm During Crises**: Crises can create panic and impulsive financial decisions, such as selling investments at the wrong time or taking on unnecessary debt. Stay calm, follow your plan, and avoid making decisions based on fear.

17.5 Long-Term Adaptability: Preparing for the Future

Financial flexibility is not just a tool for responding to current crises but also a way to prepare for the future. Throughout your life, you will go through various economic and personal stages, from income changes to new challenges and opportunities. Keeping your finances flexible will enable you to adapt successfully to these changes.

How to Maintain Financial Flexibility for the Long Term:

- **Review Your Financial Plan Regularly**: Evaluate your long-term financial plan at least once a year to ensure it remains appropriate for your current circumstances and future goals.

- **Plan for Different Scenarios**: Create different versions of your financial plan based on possible future scenarios. For example, consider how you would manage your finances in the event of a prolonged recession or a career change.

- **Save for Opportunities, Not Just Emergencies**: Maintaining adequate savings is helpful not only for facing crises but also for seizing unexpected opportunities, such as an attractive investment or a career change.

17.6 Seek Professional Help If Necessary

Financial planning can become complex, especially during times of uncertainty. If you feel you need guidance, a financial advisor can help you adjust your plan, find solutions to your concerns, and guide you in making smart decisions that enhance your financial flexibility.

Financial flexibility is essential for maintaining stability in uncertain times. By creating an emergency fund, diversifying your income, managing your debt, and maintaining a resilient mind-set, you can protect yourself from economic fluctuations and be better prepared for any challenges that arise. The key is to be proactive, adaptable, and aware of changes in both the financial environment and your personal life. With these tools, you can successfully navigate any period of uncertainty while continuing to work towards your long-term financial goals.

Chapter 18: The Importance of Financial Independence and How to Achieve It

How to Free Yourself from Financial Worries and Live on Your Own Terms

Financial independence is a state in which you have enough wealth to cover your living expenses without relying on a job or active income sources. It's one of the most sought-after goals for those who seek freedom and total control over their time and decisions. Achieving financial independence doesn't just mean reaching economic stability; it also means having the ability to live according to your own terms, free from the constant pressure of generating income to survive.

In this chapter, we'll explore what financial independence is, why it matters, and, most importantly, how you can work towards it through practical strategies and smart financial decisions.

18.1 What is Financial Independence?

Financial independence is achieved when the passive income you generate from investments, savings, or other automatic sources is enough to cover your living expenses without needing to rely on paid work. In other words, you can stop working for money if you choose to, as your generated financial resources cover your needs without requiring ongoing effort on your part.

Financial independence isn't just about accumulating a certain level of wealth; it's about reaching an economic freedom that allows you to choose how to spend your time. This doesn't necessarily mean stopping work altogether; rather, you have the freedom to decide whether you work and under what conditions.

The Pillars of Financial Independence:

- **Consistent Passive Income:** This may come from real estate investments, stock dividends, savings account interest, automated businesses, etc.

- **Controlled Living Expenses:** Financial independence requires that your expenses remain reasonable and within the limits your passive income can cover.

- **Long-Term Savings and Investment:** Achieving financial independence involves long-term financial planning, based on building assets over time that eventually generate enough income to live without active work.

18.2 Why is Financial Independence Important?

Financial independence isn't only about accumulating money. It has a deeper meaning tied to freedom of choice and control over one's life. Some of the main benefits of reaching this state include:

- **Freedom to Decide How to Use Your Time:** Financial independence allows you to devote time to what truly matters to you, whether it's spending more time with family, pursuing new projects, traveling, or engaging in creative activities.

- **Reduced Financial Stress:** Without the constant pressure to generate income to cover basic expenses, you can enjoy greater peace of mind and reduce the stress associated with financial concerns.

- **Flexibility to Make Decisions:** When you don't need to depend on a paycheck to survive, you can make decisions based on your values and personal desires, instead of being forced to accept any job or situation out of financial necessity.

- **Possibility of Early Retirement:** Many people seek financial independence as a way to retire before the traditional age, allowing them to enjoy a fulfilling life during their most productive and active years.

18.3 Strategies to Achieve Financial Independence

Achieving financial independence requires a combination of discipline, saving, investing, and long-term planning. It doesn't happen overnight, but with time and a well-thought-out strategy, you can build the resources needed to stop relying on active work.

18.3.1 Define Your Financial Independence Goal

The first step is to clearly define what financial independence means to you and how much money you'll need to achieve it. This will vary based on your lifestyle, expectations, and long-term goals.

How to Define Your Goal:

- **Calculate Your Annual Expenses:** Make a list of your current expenses and calculate how much money you'd need to live comfortably without actively working. Be sure to include not only basic expenses (housing, food, insurance) but also recreational activities, travel, and other desires.

- **Multiply by 25:** A general rule for achieving financial independence is that you should save at least 25 times your annual expenses to live off your investments. This is based on the "4% rule," which suggests that you can withdraw 4% of your investments annually without depleting your savings.

18.3.2 Increase Your Savings Rate

Your savings rate is one of the most important factors in achieving financial independence. The more you save, the faster you can invest and grow your wealth. The goal is to save and invest a significant portion of your income to accelerate your progress.

Strategies to Increase Your Savings Rate:

- **Automate Savings:** Set up automatic transfers from your income account to your savings or investment accounts. This ensures savings are made without you having to think about it.

- **Cut Unnecessary Expenses:** Evaluate your current expenses and find areas where you can cut back without sacrificing your quality of life. This might include renegotiating utility bills, reducing entertainment costs, or cutting impulsive purchases.

- **Increase Your Income:** In addition to reducing expenses, increasing your income will allow you to save more. This may involve seeking promotion opportunities, changing jobs, starting a side business, or generating additional passive income.

18.3.3 Long-Term Investing

Saving alone isn't enough to achieve financial independence. It's necessary to invest your savings so that they generate passive income and grow over time. Investing is key to making money work for you, instead of solely depending on active work.

Investment Strategies:

- **Stocks and Bonds Investments:** Investing in the stock market is one of the most effective ways to grow your wealth over the long term. A well-diversified portfolio of stocks and bonds can provide significant returns, especially if you reinvest the gains.

- **Index Funds and ETFs:** For those who prefer a more passive investment strategy, index funds or ETFs

(Exchange-Traded Funds) are ideal options. They offer automatic diversification and usually have low fees.

- **Real Estate Investments:** Buying property to rent out or resell can generate significant passive income and long-term appreciation. However, it requires careful planning and a good understanding of the real estate market.

- **Annuities or Life Insurance with Savings:** Certain financial products guarantee passive income during retirement, such as annuities. While they may have some costs, they offer the security of stable income.

18.3.4 Maintain a Frugal Yet Satisfying Lifestyle

Living below your means is one of the keys to achieving financial independence. This doesn't mean leading a life of deprivation but being mindful of your spending habits and avoiding unnecessary expenses.

How to Live Frugally Without Sacrificing Quality of Life:

- **Prioritize Experiences Over Material Goods:** Experiences, like travel or recreational activities, tend to bring more happiness and satisfaction in the long term than material possessions. Spending on what brings your personal value is more sustainable.

- **Avoid Lifestyle Inflation:** As your income increases, it can be tempting to increase your expenses as well. Controlling lifestyle inflation allows you to save more without compromising your financial goals.

- **Make Mindful Purchases:** Before buying something, ask yourself if you really need it or if it's an impulse purchase. Learning to buy with intention can prevent you from wasting money on unnecessary things.

18.3.5 Develop Multiple Sources of Passive Income

One of the keys to financial independence is having multiple sources of passive income that provide money without requiring ongoing effort. These sources may include investments in the stock market, real estate, intellectual property royalties, or income from automated businesses.

Examples of Passive Income:

- **Rental Properties:** Buying and renting properties generates monthly income without active work, provided you hire someone to manage the property.

- **Stock Dividends:** Investing in dividend-paying stocks allows you to receive regular income without selling your investments.

- **Royalties from Books, Music, or Digital Products:** If you create content such as books, music, or online courses, you can receive royalties over time, even long after the initial work is done.

- **Automated Businesses:** Creating an online business that doesn't require your constant involvement, like an automated e-commerce store, is another way to generate passive income.

18.4 The Role of Mind-set in Financial Independence

In addition to financial strategies, mind-set plays a crucial role in achieving financial independence. Developing habits of discipline, patience, and long-term vision is essential to stay on track towards economic freedom.

Mind-set for Financial Independence:

- **Have Patience:** Reaching financial independence doesn't happen quickly. It takes time and consistency. Maintain a long-term vision and don't get discouraged if progress is slow.

- **Be Disciplined:** Self-discipline is essential to maintain your savings and investment habits, especially when it's tempting to spend on unnecessary things or get distracted from your goals.

- **Keep Emotions in Check:** Markets and personal life can be volatile. Stay calm during market fluctuations and avoid making financial decisions based on fear or greed.

18.5 Adjust Your Plan Over Time

Your path to financial independence won't be linear. There will be times when you need to adjust your plan based on changes in your life, your goals, or the economic environment. Keep flexibility and be willing to modify your strategies as needed.

How to Adjust Your Plan:

- **Periodically Review Your Investments:** As you age or circumstances change, adjust your investment portfolio to reflect your new risk and return needs.

- **Increase Your Savings Contributions:** If you receive a raise or find a new income source, consider increasing your saving and investment rate to accelerate your path to financial independence.

- **Reevaluate Your Goals:** As you get closer to your financial goals, it's essential to review and adjust them according to your current situation. You may find that you can live with less than you initially expected.

Financial independence is one of the most empowering and liberating goals you can achieve. It not only allows you to live without the pressure of working for money but also gives you the freedom to make decisions based on your true desires and values.

Through a combination of disciplined saving, intelligent investing, and developing passive income streams, you can build a future where you have complete control over your time and finances. The journey to financial independence may be long, but with perseverance and a solid plan, it's entirely achievable.

Chapter 19: Long-Term Wealth Preservation Strategies

How to Protect and Grow Your Assets with a Future-Oriented Vision

Achieving financial independence is an important milestone, but maintaining and growing that wealth over time requires a solid investment strategy. The decisions you make at this stage will be crucial in protecting your assets and ensuring they continue to generate passive income for you and future generations. Long-term investing is not only about preserving what you have accomplished but also ensuring steady growth that allows you to enjoy a comfortable life free from financial worries.

In this chapter, we'll explore long-term investment strategies to help you safeguard your wealth, minimize risk, and ensure your money continues to work for you. We'll also examine the importance of diversification, risk management, and how to adjust your portfolio over time to maximize gains and minimize losses.

19.1 The Importance of Long-Term Investing

Long-term investing is based on the idea that markets tend to grow over time, even if there are temporary fluctuations. Long-term investments allow you to take advantage of compound interest, continuous asset growth, and reduced risk as time smooths out market fluctuations.

A long-term investment strategy not only helps grow your wealth but also protects you from impulsive decisions that can arise in response to market fluctuations. Maintaining a long-term vision allows you to avoid panic and benefit from growth opportunities that only reveal themselves over time.

Advantages of Long-Term Investing:

- **Reduced Impact of Volatility:** While markets may experience short-term fluctuations, the long-term trend is usually upward. Holding onto your investments over a longer period helps you weather volatile periods.

- **Compound Interest:** By reinvesting your gains, your investments generate additional returns, accelerating your wealth growth. The longer you invest, the greater the effect of compound interest.

- **Lower Costs:** Long-term investing generally involves fewer transactions, reducing costs associated with frequent buying and selling of assets, such as commissions and taxes.

19.2 Diversification: The Key to Protecting Your Wealth

One of the fundamental rules of long-term investing is diversification. Diversification means spreading your money across different types of assets, industries, sectors, and regions, reducing the risk that a single poor investment will significantly impact your wealth. Diversification helps balance risk and return, ensuring that if one sector or asset loses value, others may offset those losses.

How to Diversify Your Portfolio:

- **Invest in Multiple Asset Classes:** Invest in a mix of stocks, bonds, real estate, mutual funds, and ETFs to reduce risk. Each asset type responds differently to market conditions, so a balanced mix can smooth out fluctuations.

- **Geographic Diversification:** Don't limit your investments to one country or region. Investing in international markets can increase growth opportunities and protect you from the volatility of a single market.

- **Sector Diversification:** Ensure your investments are spread across different sectors of the economy (technology, healthcare, real estate, energy, etc.). This protects you from significant declines in any single sector.

19.3 Investment Strategies to Preserve Wealth

There are several long-term investment strategies ideal for those looking to maintain and grow their wealth. These strategies are designed to maximize returns over time and minimize unnecessary risks.

19.3.1 Growth Stock Investing

Growth stocks are those from companies that are expanding and have the potential to generate significant returns over time. While they tend to be more volatile in the short term, growth stocks often yield high returns in the long term. Technology companies and innovative businesses are often examples of growth stocks.

Advantages:

- **High Return Potential:** Growing companies generally reinvest their profits to expand, which can lead to significant appreciation in stock prices.

- **Long-Term Benefit:** While growth stocks may experience temporary drops, their long-term trend is often positive.

Considerations:

- **Higher Short-Term Risk:** Growth stocks can be volatile and more sensitive to market fluctuations, so it's important to maintain a long-term outlook and be willing to endure short-term volatility.

19.3.2 Dividend Investing

Dividend-paying stocks are an excellent choice for generating consistent passive income while also protecting and growing your wealth. Companies that pay dividends regularly distribute a portion of their profits to shareholders, providing you with a stable income without needing to sell your shares.

Advantages:

- **Steady Income:** Dividends provide a passive income stream that you can reinvest or use to cover expenses without selling assets.
- **Stability:** Companies that pay dividends tend to be more stable and less volatile, as they are often established companies with positive cash flows.

Considerations:

- **Moderate Growth:** While dividend-paying companies tend to be more stable, their stock price growth may be slower than that of growth stocks.

19.3.3 Bond Investing

Bonds are a key investment for any long-term portfolio, offering security and predictable returns. Bonds are essentially loans you provide to governments or companies in exchange for regular interest payments and the principal value of the bond upon maturity.

Advantages:

- **Security:** Bonds are less volatile than stocks and offer regular income through interest payments.

- **Risk Diversification:** Bonds can act as a counterbalance to stocks in your portfolio, reducing overall risk, especially during recessions.

Considerations:
- **Lower Returns:** While bonds are safer, they generally offer lower returns than stocks, which may limit your wealth growth.

19.3.4 Real Estate Investments

Investing in real estate is an effective strategy to preserve and grow your wealth, as real estate tends to appreciate over time and can generate passive income through rental properties. Additionally, real estate offers protection against inflation, as prices generally increase over time.

Advantages:
- **Passive Income:** By renting out properties, you can generate consistent income while your asset appreciates in value.
- **Capital Appreciation:** Over time, real estate values tend to rise, generating profits when you decide to sell.

Considerations:
- **Active Management:** Investing in real estate may require active management, especially if you rent out properties. It also involves additional costs like maintenance, taxes, and insurance.

19.3.5 Index Funds and ETFs

Index funds and ETFs (Exchange-Traded Funds) are passive investments that track the performance of a market index, like the S&P 500. They are ideal for long-term investors seeking instant diversification at low fees.

Advantages:

- **Low Cost:** Index funds and ETFs generally have lower fees compared to actively managed funds.
- **Automatic Diversification:** By investing in an index fund or ETF, you automatically diversify your investment across many companies or assets.

Considerations:

- **Market Dependence:** Since these funds track an index, their performance depends directly on the overall market. If the market declines, the fund is likely to decline as well.

19.4 Risk Management: Protecting Your Wealth

Risk management is essential to preserving your wealth over the long term. While it's important to grow your investments, protecting your assets from unforeseen losses is equally crucial.

Risk Management Strategies:

- **Maintain Proper Diversification:** Diversification is the most effective way to manage risk. Ensure your portfolio is balanced across different asset classes, sectors, and geographic regions.
- **Establish an Emergency Fund:** Before taking on significant investment risks, make sure you have a solid emergency fund covering at least six months of expenses. This will allow you to avoid selling investments during a crisis.
- **Assess Your Risk Tolerance:** As you age or your circumstances change, it's essential to adjust your portfolio to reflect your risk tolerance. If you're approaching retirement, you may want to reduce exposure to more volatile investments.

- **Avoid Trying to Time the Market:** Attempting to predict market highs and lows is usually a risky and ineffective strategy. Instead, adopt a long-term approach, invest consistently, and avoid making decisions based on panic or euphoria.

19.5 Adjusting Your Portfolio Over Time

Your investment portfolio should not be static. As your circumstances change, whether due to age, shifts in financial goals, or market fluctuations, you should adjust your portfolio to reflect your new situation.

How to Adjust Your Portfolio Over Time:

- **Rebalance Periodically:** Rebalancing involves adjusting your portfolio to ensure that asset allocation remains aligned with your goals. If one asset type has grown significantly, you may need to sell some of that investment and reinvest in other assets to maintain balance.

- **Shift Strategy with Life Stage:** As you approach retirement, it's wise to move some of your investments into safer assets, like bonds or dividend-paying stocks, to reduce risk.

- **Consider New Opportunities:** Financial markets are constantly evolving. Stay informed about new investment opportunities, such as emerging technologies, renewable energy, or cryptocurrencies, but always with an appropriate risk management strategy.

19.6 The Importance of Continued Financial Education

Investing is a constantly changing field, and staying informed is essential for making wise decisions over time. Devoting time to continuous financial education will allow you to adapt to new trends, investment tools, and changes in the economic environment.

How to Keep Learning:

- **Read Books and Articles on Finance and Investing:** There are numerous books and blogs written by experts that can help you better understand the world of investing.

- **Consult Financial Advisors:** If you lack the confidence or time to manage your portfolio, working with a financial advisor can be an excellent option to protect and grow your wealth.

- **Attend Seminars and Conferences:** Participating in financial events and online seminars can offer you new perspectives and investment strategies.

Maintaining and growing your wealth over the long term requires a combination of intelligent investment strategies, prudent risk management, and a long-term vision. By diversifying, investing in assets aligned with your goals, and constantly evaluating your portfolio, you can ensure that your wealth not only remains intact but continues to grow over time. The key is to maintain patience, discipline, and adaptability, adjusting your strategy according to market conditions and your own financial evolution.

Chapter 20: From Financial Security to Building a Lasting Legacy

How to Ensure Your Wealth and Values Endure for Future Generations

Once you've achieved financial security, the next step is considering how your wealth, values, and teachings can transcend time. True financial success isn't just about accumulating wealth to enjoy throughout life but also leaving a lasting legacy that benefits future generations, whether that's family, community, or society as a whole. Creating a legacy goes beyond simply transferring wealth; it also involves passing down values, principles, and a forward-looking vision.

In this final chapter, we'll explore how you can go beyond financial security to start thinking about building a lasting legacy, from estate planning to philanthropy. This chapter will also guide you on how to balance wealth management with teaching financial responsibility to your heirs, ensuring that your legacy is not only preserved but also valued and wisely managed.

20.1 What Is a Financial Legacy?

A financial legacy isn't just about leaving a sum of money for your heirs. It refers to how your actions, financial decisions, and values will impact future generations. Your legacy may encompass:

- **Transfer of Financial Assets:** This includes real estate, investments, savings, and other tangible assets that will be passed on to your heirs.

- **Values and Financial Education:** A financial legacy also involves teaching your children and grandchildren the importance of financial management, saving, investing, and responsible decision-making.

- **Social Impact and Philanthropy:** Your legacy can include significant contributions to charitable causes, nonprofits, or projects that reflect your values and beliefs.

20.2 Estate Planning: How to Protect Your Legacy

One of the key elements of creating a lasting legacy is effective estate planning. Without a clear plan, your assets may not be distributed as you wish, or your heirs could face legal, tax, or family issues. Estate planning ensures that your assets reach the people or causes of your choice in the most efficient manner possible.

Essential Components of Estate Planning:

- **Updated Will:** A will is the foundation of any estate plan. Ensure it is up-to-date and reflects your current wishes regarding asset distribution.

- **Trusts:** Trusts are useful tools for managing the distribution of your assets. They can help avoid lengthy legal processes and protect your assets from high taxes or mismanagement.

- **Clearly Designated Beneficiaries:** Make sure all your accounts, insurance policies, and assets with designated beneficiaries (such as retirement accounts) are up-to-date and aligned with your estate plan.

- **Minimizing Estate Taxes:** Work with a financial advisor or estate planning attorney to reduce the tax burden on your estate, ensuring that your heirs receive the majority of your assets.

0.3 Teaching Financial Responsibility to Future Generations

Leaving a financial inheritance is only part of the equation. Without the necessary education and tools, your heirs may not be able to manage and preserve your legacy effectively. Teaching financial responsibility is essential to ensure the wealth you leave is used intelligently and productively.

How to Teach Financial Responsibility:

- **Start Early:** Involve your children or grandchildren in conversations about money from a young age. Teach them the value of saving, investing, and avoiding unnecessary debt.

- **Lead by Example:** Your actions speak louder than words. If you demonstrate financial discipline, your heirs are likely to manage money similarly.

- **Encourage Entrepreneurship and Financial Independence:** Encourage your children to develop entrepreneurial skills and work towards their own financial independence. This will provide them with the tools to grow and protect the wealth they inherit.

- **Consider an Educational Trust:** If you're concerned your heirs may not be ready to inherit a large sum, you can establish a trust that limits access to the funds until they reach certain educational or financial maturity milestones.

20.4 Philanthropy: Leaving a Positive Impact on Society

One of the most meaningful ways to create a lasting legacy is through philanthropy. While it's important to leave an inheritance for your family, you may also wish to allocate part of your wealth to causes you care about. Not only does this contribute to making the world a better place, but it can also inspire your heirs to continue your philanthropic efforts.

Options for Philanthropy:

- **Direct Donations:** You can make direct donations to charitable organizations during your lifetime or leave instructions in your will to allocate part of your estate to specific causes.

- **Charitable Trusts:** Charitable trusts allow you to donate a portion of your assets to a nonprofit organization while still retaining control over how those funds are used.

- **Family Foundations:** If you want to create a more enduring impact, consider establishing a family foundation to fund projects and organizations over time. This can also involve future generations of your family in managing the philanthropic legacy.

20.5 Balancing Financial Planning with Family Values

Creating a lasting legacy isn't just about transferring wealth but also about passing down values and principles. It's essential that your financial plan reflects the ideals and beliefs you've cultivated throughout your life. This includes not only teaching your heirs to manage money but also to live by the values you've practiced.

How to Pass on Values Along with Wealth:

- **Draft a Legacy Document:** In addition to your will, consider writing a letter or document that explains your wishes and values to your heirs. This document can include life lessons, the importance of generosity, and the responsible management of wealth.

- **Involve Your Family in Estate Planning:** Allow your heirs to participate in decisions about the future of the family estate, including its use for philanthropic works or investments. This will not only instill a greater sense of responsibility but also ensure alignment with your values.

- **Encourage Teamwork:** Foster a sense of unity around managing the family estate. This helps create a shared legacy that can be protected and grown across multiple generations.

20.6 Ongoing Review and Adjustment of the Legacy

Your legacy plan is not something to set up once and forget. Over time, your circumstances and goals may change, so it's essential to review and adjust your plan periodically. As you grow older, your perspective on the legacy you wish to leave may shift, and new opportunities may arise to enhance or expand your impact.

When to Review Your Plan:

- **Changes in Your Family Situation:** Events like marriage, the birth of a child, or the loss of a loved one may require adjustments to your estate plan.

- **Changes in Tax Laws:** Tax and inheritance laws change over time. Stay informed about these changes to ensure your plan remains tax-efficient.

- **Reevaluating Philanthropic Goals:** As you grow, you may discover new causes that inspire you. Review your charitable contributions and ensure they align with your current values and priorities.

20.7 Leaving a Lasting Impact

A true legacy isn't measured solely by the money you leave behind but by the lasting impact your actions and values have on people's lives and society. Creating a meaningful legacy means thinking not only about the financial well-being of your heirs but also about how you can contribute to a better world.

By ensuring your heirs receive a solid financial education, aligning your wealth with your values, and considering the philanthropic impact you can have, you'll be building a legacy that endures far beyond your life. This legacy will not only benefit future generations of your family but also leave a positive mark on the world.

Conclusion of the Book:

Financial security and building a lasting legacy are goals that go far beyond merely generating wealth. By making wise decisions, building a solid financial foundation, and passing on values to your heirs, you can ensure that your impact endures for generations. From disciplined saving and strategic investing to estate planning and philanthropy, each step you take brings you closer not only to a freer, more fulfilling life but also to a legacy that reflects your principles and beliefs.

This book has provided you with a comprehensive roadmap for improving your personal finances, achieving financial independence, and building a lasting legacy. Now it's up to you to apply these strategies in your life, take control of your financial future, and ensure that your influence benefits those around you, both now and in the future. With discipline, vision, and responsibility, the financial future you desire is within reach.

www.ingramcontent.com/pod-product-compliance
Lightning Source LLC
Chambersburg PA
CBHW052210220526
45471CB00004B/1893